In the Trenches

In Search of the Counselor Within

Experience-based Strategies for Today's School Counselor

Robin Adair Di Peppe

Dedication

To my amazing husband and best friend, Arch
for his unwavering love and support
and
to my two wonderful children, Shannon and Joe
who continue to bring me so much joy

Acknowledgments

I would like to thank Lenny Cascio, Roxanne Johnson, and Susan Biggs for sharing their time, expertise, and suggestions in the editing of this book. I would also like to thank Paula Williams for giving me the chance to return to my middle schools roots once again before I retired and for teaching me to not take myself quite so seriously. I would also like to thank Marguerite Shiffler for her helpful suggestions.

Above all, I would like to thank all of them for their honesty, support, and enduring friendship throughout the years.

TABLE OF CONTENTS

CHAPTER 26

CHAPTER 27

CHAPTER 28

CHAPTER 29

CHAPTER 30

Chapter 1: Disclaimer

"The time has come," the Walrus said,
To talk of many things:
Of shoes—and ships—and sealing wax—
Of cabbages and kings—
And why the sea is boiling hot—
And whether pigs have wings."

<u>Through the Looking Glass</u>
Lewis Carroll

On June 29, 2007, I closed the door to my office in the Counseling Department for the final time and walked slowly with my friend Roxanne, the Counseling Director, towards the front door of the school. We met the sixth grade principal Dawn on her way down the hall of the now empty school and a casual conversation regarding school details began between the two women. I didn't enter into the conversation because I was now considered a "retiree." I listened and smiled as we rounded the corner by the main office. The conversation continued, even after we had reached the front door.

By nature, or perhaps necessity, women are good communicators and know how to fill moments that can be awkward. After hugging Roxanne and telling her that we would get together for dinner over the summer and promising Dawn that I would come back to visit, I swung open the door and, without looking back, walked down the sidewalk to my car, which was parked near the flagpole. After depositing my final packed cardboard box onto the back seat, I slid into the front seat, put my key in the ignition, and then looked back at the school. My hands were on the steering wheel, but I let them slide down into my lap, and I suddenly leaned back in my seat.

As the event of my retirement had grown closer during the previous weeks, I had wondered how I would feel when I finally closed the last chapter of my career in education. I had been so busy with all of the details that a school counselor must do to close out a school year that I hadn't had too many moments to dwell on the subject. Now as I sat in the driver's seat of the car, my mind did a quick rewind of the tape. I shouldn't have been all that surprised, I suppose. Whenever we make big transitions in our lives, we tend to take a glance at the big picture before we let go of the past and move on.

People who claim to have had a Near Death Experience report to have had their entire life flash before them in an instant---all of the people, events, joys, and sorrows flowing like a constant and unbroken wave down the river of time. I cannot say that my feelings were that dramatic or spontaneous, but my mind did skip all the way back to my first teaching job in 1975 in a middle school in the east end of Henrico County, which borders the City of Richmond, Virginia.

Over the next ten minutes or so, memories of the last three decades glided quietly through my mind. I had worked in city schools, county schools, and rural schools--- the first fifteen years as an English teacher and the last sixteen as a school counselor—basically, my entire life had been spent inside school walls, either as a student or as an educator. I had taught English, as well as been a school counselor for every grade between sixth and twelfth. I had taught alongside many gifted teachers and counselors and been extremely fortunate to work with four dynamic and highly professional Counseling Directors (in chronological order: Lenny, Susan, Paula, and Roxanne), who unconditionally shared their insight and knowledge with me—individuals whose very presence had been a model of what a good counselor should be. I had experienced moments of supreme joy and fulfillment that only teaching and working with children can bring. I had also experienced what I perceived to be disappoint-ments and sometimes failures regarding things that I had wanted so much to happen at the time but that were destined not to be. My measuring stick for myself has always been a particularly long and tough one.

Yet now as my mind did a quick review of all of those years, they really did join together as a single strand forever embedded in time, and at that moment, I had a gentle but deep epiphany: all things considered, I had accomplished exactly what I had set out to do from the day I walked out of college until the day I had walked out of this school, and I was content. I then turned the key in the ignition, backed up, and drove away without fear or a backward glance to begin the next chapter of my life.

****

This book is not about me, nor will it be filled with extensive educational research or documented studies. It will be the journey of one person through the gardens, and sometimes land mines, that a career in education can generate. My purpose is to present to you what I learned over the decades: what worked and what didn't work, how times changed and how people didn't, what I gained and what I lost, and how we bring ourselves to our job. Some-times you may want to accuse me of being brutally honest and wonder if I became jaded. I didn't—just realistic. Experience will do that, you know.

My journey is not your journey. However, I hope that in sharing the experiences that I had with children, parents, teachers, administrators, and other school counselors, I can weave a thread of commonalities that we all share in search for our identity and a sense of balance in both our career, as well as our personal life because, like it or not, both will intersect. Finding the balance will be your greatest survival skill.

Since my career choices allowed me to experience the viewpoints of both a teacher and a school counselor, and because administrators and teachers can play an integral part in your decision-making process sometimes, I hope to be able to offer you an unbiased perspective of how all of these roles will interconnect on a ongoing basis in your efforts to help children.

The individual examples of children and school interactions will not be recognizable to the individuals to whom they refer. I have intermixed both counseling and teaching experiences, as well as changed ages, gender, grade levels, and in some cases, blended identities to protect people's privacy. Some situations that I describe will be generic, even if they appear to be somewhat specific or age-related. My hope is to touch upon as many possible and probable scenarios for those of you who are either a new counselor or an evolving one.

I have also chosen to write this book in conversational English (you may find a preposition at the end of a sentence!) and direct the message to **you** as if we are sitting together at a table drinking a cup of coffee. This means that I will not be hard and fast with the grammar rules of English, which can sometimes sound very stilted. I will also choose to speak of a student as either "he" or "she" for the fluidity of a sentence. The use of he or she will always mean either/or.

Whether you are called in your school district a professional school counselor, school counselor, or guidance counselor (all three titles still exist), it is up to you to find your own vision and goals in your career. Know thoroughly the rules and counselor ethics as stated in the Handbook of the American School Counselor Association (ASCA). Know the regulations of both your school system and the goals and expectations of your individual school. Although you may sometimes feel that your vision may be limited by guidelines that are not of your making, remember that those lines have been drawn in the sand to protect both you and the lives of those who you may impact in both the short term and long term.

These circumstances need not limit your vision. They are the framework that will encompass all that you are and will bring to this career that you have chosen. Try not to lose perspective, but always keep your vision alive.

Chapter 2: Why Be a Counselor?

"Life is just a mirror, and what you see out there, you must first see inside of you."

Wally "Famous" Amos
Actor, Writer, and Cookie
Man

I am aware that to ask someone why he or she wants to be a counselor may appear somewhat trite in that it is the most obvious and expected question to ask in a book like this. There is only one heart-felt and educational reason, right? We all tend to answer this question in basically the same way. Notice that I am not answering the question.

The truth is that there are as many answers to this "why" as there are people who choose this profession. However, it is the most important question that you will ever ask yourself in your career, and it is important that you are truthful with yourself from day one when you answer it. It is, and will be, the foundation block upon which you stand and dictate how you think, feel, and respond to others in your daily life both inside and outside of school. There will always be run off into your personal life. I am devoting an entire chapter to that one!

If it appears that I am suddenly taking on a jaded tone, I really am not. What I am being is realistic. As in any profession, people have personal agendas for most of the things that they do. No matter how idealistic and sincere we are, we bring ourselves to the process. We can't escape being human. I have known counselors whose heart, mind, and very soul are driven to help others. Their love for children is deep and abiding. They are on a mission to make life better for those who have a need.

On the other hand, I have also known people who became a counselor because they either wanted to get out of the classroom or had no desire to go into one in the first place except to get certified. You must be very clear with yourself about your true intentions. Counseling is not for the faint of heart. It takes a lot of hard work and often personal soul searching if you want to do the job well. You can't wing it when you are dealing with people's lives. Your words will have an influence on those who come to you for help. How you present your thoughts to them can have either a positive or negative effect, or some-time no effect at all, but this is usually when a child is forced to see you. Resistance can only be overcome by persistence. Put on your battle gear. That one is coming your way, for sure.

The bottom line is this: whatever your reason or motivation is for becoming a counselor, use this choice as a springboard for helping others and yourself to grow in understanding and hope, as we all learn to cope in a world that presents untold challenges to everyone in our daily lives. Each time you touch the life of another, you will find a place in yourself that has room to grow, as well.

Chapter 3: What Graduate School Can and Cannot Teach You

"Experience is the child of Thought, and Thought is the child of Action. We cannot learn men from books."

> Benjamin Disraeli, Earl of
> Beaconsfield

I love books. It is one of the reasons why I originally became an English teacher. Books can take us to places that we may never visit, inspire us to be better people, make us confront hidden emotions, and touch our lives in ways that can't easily be put into words. What books cannot do, however, is give us experiences that can only be learned through the act of living.

As with learning anything new, laying a strong foundation built on knowledge is the first step before we should attempt any new or difficult task. That is what graduate school is all about. Theory, ethics, method, child development, human behavior, and sensitivity to multiculturalism are just some of the tools that we need to collect in order to eventually do our job. It is during your practicum and/or internship, though, that you are finally allowed to get your feet wet under the supervision of a mentor before you will be set free to brave the world of school counseling on your own.

It is during this learning experience that we begin to get an inkling that what we learned from books and classroom discussions will not always transfer neatly into some of the real life situations that we are going to confront. What we were taught can help us decide what framework that we will use to respond, and it can give us insight into the developmental and emotional levels of the child. However, there can be multiple variations on a theme, and each one will have its own set of circumstances with unique twists and turns. Even though it may run along a common theme of the expected issues, such as divorce, family conflict, grades, personality conflicts with others in the school environment, and loss of a loved one, there is no standard fix for any of these.

Whether you are counseling an elementary, middle, or high school student, it is imperative that you understand that whatever the issue is that led the child to your office, that child has already been prejudiced by his individual personality, level of development, family construct, positive and negative experiences, and, yes, genetics, before he even reached your door. Remember this when you hit the proverbial wall and wonder if the child is listening to you at all or if you can even make a dent in his understanding of the situation and his role in it. The truth is that he might have just come to your office to vent, not to be shown reason or to get help. That's okay. Better to let the child have a safe place to complain, whine, cry, or explode without disrupting class or saying something to the teacher that is likely to get him into bigger trouble than he may already be in. Reason will not always work in the face of human emotion, and it will not have a chance at all if you don't let the child let out his frustration, anger, hurt, or pain before you try to confront the issue. Otherwise, you may as well be talking to a fence post.

This is when your book knowledge, listening skills, reading of body language, patience, instinct, and sometimes just plain horse sense will all need to converge to get as accurate a picture as possible of what is really the underlying problem. We can't be expected to be psychic, and if a child won't open up, don't feel that you have failed. There are children of all ages who will choose to hide their real feelings, only tell part of the truth, flat out lie, or try to manipulate a situation, either for self-protection or because that is what they have learned to do at home.

In addition, there will be many times that children are upset and honestly don't know what is bothering them because it isn't just one thing. Sometimes it is a cluster of situations that have happened in close proximity that have finally pushed the child over the edge. It is the classic example on the one too many drops of water in the glass which caused it to finally overflow.

It will be your job to help the child untangle it all by getting him to verbally identify and separate each situation brick by brick in order to tear down the wall of frustration or anger that he has built. It may take time and a lot of determination on your part, but once you can get him to name individual instances that have caused him to finally feel overwhelmed, you will be able to deal with each one and hopefully find ways to either alleviate the stress, solve at least some of the problems, and then teach coping skills for those issues that will be ongoing.

These are the skills that only experience can teach. As you practice over time, you will accumulate a repertoire of skills and possible options that you have found have a pretty good success rate in working with your counselees. However, keep in mind that what works for one child may not work for another, even if the situations are similar. Each child will respond according to his own personality and emotional construct, so collect as many strategies as you can and don't throw out any idea that may have merit, even if it hasn't worked for you in the past. It may well work for you with the next child who walks in the door when all other options have failed.

My wonderful Italian father-in-law once gave me the best parenting advice that I ever received: "You've got to be smarter than the kid." You have the knowledge, so listen, observe, and give it your best effort. Sometimes, you will just have to plain outlast them.

Chapter 4: Know Yourself: Dealing with Your "Old Dirt" First

"Know then thyself, presume not God to scan,
The proper study of mankind is man."

Alexander Pope, "Essay on Man"

This is not an easy subject for anyone. In the book <u>When the Legends Die</u> by Hal Borland, the main character Thomas asks his mother Bessie, a Native American, what the meaning is of the stripes down the back of a chipmunk's tail. She tells him that the stripes are the paths from its eyes, with which it sees now and tomorrow, to its tail, which is always behind it and a part of yesterday. "When you are a man," she says, "you will have a tail, though you will never see it. You will have something always behind you." To live is to create a past which is always with us.

Although we do not keep our good or bad memories in the forefront of our mind everyday, they still have become a part of the tapestry of our life and helped to fashion each of us as a unique human being. You will discover how true this is one day if you are ever confronted with a particular situation that touches an emotional memory buried deep within you, and it can blindside you before you can even think. Here is my personal example, and although I understand why it happened, I am not proud of it.

One day a student came into my office and told me that there was a girl in the bathroom who was crying. I thanked her and went straight to the restroom to find out what had happened. The girl really didn't want to talk about it, but I convinced her that she couldn't stay in the bathroom all day and to allow me to try to help her deal with whatever the issue was. She finally told me that her boyfriend had just backed her into a wall and slapped her in the face. She was unhurt, but before I could blink, I felt a rage rise in me that I didn't even know existed. Why? Because at the age of six, I had witnessed an act of domestic violence within my own family, and it had left a profound impression on me.

So, flashing back to the girl in the bathroom, I got livid and demanded that she take me to her boyfriend. I didn't have to go far. He was hovering nearby in the hallway. I then proceeded to lose my cool, as well as every counseling skill that I had ever acquired. I told him that he better never lay a hand in anger on her or any other girl again and marched the both of them down to the assistant principal's office. Unfortunately, it didn't end there. I pretty much went into a tirade about his behavior, verbally jumping on him for doing it and her for taking it. The administrator blanched, and I could tell that he thought that I had totally lost my mind. Maybe I had for a minute. I then walked out of the office, leaving the administrator to decide whatever consequences that he saw fit to resolve this situation. Awhile later, when I finally got my sanity back, I was horrified by my reaction and apologized to both children separately for my angry outburst, and then I counseled them both. Afterwards, I went directly back to see the administrator who looked at me almost fearfully and said, "What was that all about?"

I was very lucky that this man had known me for many years because he would have been justified in placing a Letter of Reprimand in my permanent file for my behavior. I knew that I owed him an explanation, so I again traveled back for the second time that day to a memory that I would love to forget and told him my personal story. He seemed relieved and understood why it had happened. I profoundly apologized, while I assured him that it would never happen again, and it never did.

After the incident, I spent some time searching myself for any other "emotional triggers" that might have the potential to cause me to lose perspective. It can be tough to revisit old wounds, but it is necessary if you are going to keep your objectivity as a counselor. You owe it to yourself, and you really owe it to the children and the others who you will counsel. You will be less effective in your job if you don't.

I am not suggesting that you have to drag yourself down to visit every dark place in your soul before you become a school counselor. To do that could make you become a very self-absorbed person, and we all know that no one lives a charmed life. What I am saying is that it is important that you take some time to look at your own emotional construct and the major events, good and bad, that have had the biggest influences in making you who you are. We all have pressure points that can set us off, mostly based on a combination of personality and personal experiences. There will always be places in you that will be sore to the touch. We can't change what has already happened, but we can control our reaction to those events, if we become aware of them before they jump out in front of us unexpectedly from around some shadowy corner of our mind. If you can't do this, you haven't really come to terms with that particular personal issue, and you must. If you can't do it alone, talk to someone who can help you gain perspective.

As human beings, emotion tends to get the first bite out of us before logic puts on the leash. You may be a school counselor, but you will always be a human being first. The more you visit yourself, the more self-aware you will become. Knowing your own vulnerable places will save you from what can be some very embarrassing moments in your career. Hopefully, they won't come out in the unexpected and extreme way that mine did, but so many things, even small things, can inadvertently set us off. It comes with the territory because we deal with emotionally charged issues everyday. It can psychologically wear us down and expose hidden kinks in our own armor.

If you find that some internal anger or hurt does get the best of you, don't think that you have "lost face." Step up to the plate, correct the situation, and always carry an apology in your pocket. If people are going to judge you for being human, then they need to confront their own demons. Everyone has shadow places. Believe it or not, it was confronting the issues in my own past that helped me to become a better and more empathetic counselor. By becoming aware of my own emotional construct and both the positive and negative events that had influenced my perspective on life, I explored and found better ways to teach coping skills to children who were experiencing difficult times in their lives.

You will always take yourself to your counseling. Objectivity is the goal, but it will sometimes be a struggle. When you find yourself letting emotion dominate over objectivity, sit back, take a breath, count to ten until you get your sense of control back, and then rephrase your words before you say something that you may regret. We sometimes use the technique of *silence* to wait for a student to respond. A moment of silence can work for us, too. It will give you enough time to become aware and regroup your thoughts so that you can get back on track and off of your own emotional roller coaster.

Again, it is better if you will look for these potential emotional land mines before you begin your counseling career, but sometimes we just sail right past them, deceiving ourselves that they are not a problem. No matter how much soul-searching you do, there is always a potential for one of these unforgiving ghosts to come back and haunt you when you least expect it. If this should happen, grab that memory by the throat and instantly remind yourself that you cannot allow your life experiences to prejudice your thinking. The words you choose must give the child or adult clear and objective strategies for them to consider as they struggle with whatever the problem is. You will have to deal with your own emotions later. It may be tough, but you have no other option. Sometimes you may have to face your own internal challenges at unexpected and inopportune moments, but it is imperative that you recognize them, come to terms with those conflicted feelings, and learn to cope with them. As I said earlier in this book, being a counselor is not for the faint-hearted.

In the final analysis, you must heal your own wounds before you can be of help to others. You cannot be an example of the "walking wounded." We are all warned about this in graduate school. The best suggestion I can give you is to reiterate what Wally "Famous Amos," of chocolate chip cookie fame once said,

"Life is just a mirror, and what you see out there, you must first see inside of you."

Chapter 5: The Three Sides of Compassion

"Compassion brings us to a stop, and for a moment we rise above ourselves."

Mason Cooley,
American Aphorist and
Professor Emeritus of English,
Speech, and World
Literature at the College of
Staten Island

I suppose you could say that I have a disagreement with Webster's International Dictionary. In looking up a standard definition for *compassion*, the dictionary groups it with *sympathy* and *pity*. I do agree that the feeling of compassion is "a fellowship in feeling." Why do I appear to be nit-picking over the definition? Let me explain.

There are degrees within each emotion, but emotion itself cannot neatly be subdivided. When we are sitting in our office listening to a child, a myriad of emotions can simultaneously surface within us during the course of a single conversation. How we initially react to what we are being told has more to do with our own experiences and mindset than it does with what the child or parent is relaying to us.

Compassion is one of our most common responses as a school counselor. For many counselors it is directly rooted to why we chose to be in this profession. If you don't have it, you cannot relate to the humanity in yourself or others. Without it, objectivity has no balance, and you will be unable to reach that part of a person that can be influenced, for change comes through making both a mental and emotional connection with an idea.

We can't always make a hard and fast distinction with the feeling of compassion because how we interpret this feeling depends on our individual emotional construct. Since we should view Webster's definition as accurate, then I contend that each of the synonyms for this feeling should be viewed as degrees (my personal interpretation).

As for *sympathy*, I view it as a feeling of sorrow for someone while not necessarily making a deep connection with the circumstances. Either you have never experienced the situation yourself and, therefore, may not relate, or your objectivity may be sending you a signal that this person is not so much a victim of circumstances as someone who continues to make negative choices again and again.

I view *compassion* as a much deeper feeling. You can identify with the pain because you have experienced that same feeling, even if the circumstances may have been different. For example, whether a relative, friend, colleague, or pet has died, you know what the pain of a deep loss feels like. Loss is a global human feeling. You can feel true compassion for that person because that feeling connects straight to your heart.

Now we come to *pity*. Personally, I have trouble with this one. Pity to me is an unnecessary extreme. I view pity as an unconstructive response to a situation because it sends a message of helplessness. It means that the situation is hopeless and nothing can be done, and it can open the door to emotional self-indulgence and victimhood. I don't believe in hopelessness, and I don't think counselors should tolerate this feeling in themselves or inadvertently teach it to others. Believe me, I am not being idealistic, and I don't live in a fool's dream. There are numerous circumstances that are beyond our control, but helping someone come to terms with what is or what has happened defies the need for pity and teaches the life skill of *empowerment*.

I know that some of you will disagree with me, but I stand firm and make no apologies for my opinion on this issue. Pity can blind your ability to help a child or adult deal with or find solutions to make a set of circumstances better or at least less painful over time. You cannot afford to grovel in this emotion, or you will not be as effective a counselor as you could be. Compassion used wisely is one of your strongest tools. If used unwisely, it may enable a child and often his parent to believe that they are trapped under a NO EXIT sign with little or no way out.

Sympathy will come easily. Compassion will come with a heart connection. However, pity, although well-meant, should be only a momentary emotion that is recognized and felt like touching a hot stove. Jump back and reach for compassion instead. It will better serve both you and those you are counseling. Perhaps it is best said by the Dalai Lama: "If you want others to be happy, practice compassion. If you want to be happy, practice compassion."

Chapter 6: Leave your Worries on the Doorstep: Separating School from Home

"Worry is like a rocking chair: It gives you something to do, but it doesn't get you anywhere."

Erma Bombeck
God's Little Devotional Book for
Mothers

Although the necessity of separating your school life from your home life seems to be a no-brainer, I have found that knowing this and doing this are two entirely different things. Why? Because we are human beings with personal lives first and counselors second. It just can't be any other way.

I suppose that there may be a fortunate few out there who can turn off their home life like the flip of a switch the minute they cross the threshold of the school, but I was not one of them. Most of us carry a laundry list of personal concerns, expectations, and responsibilities with us from the moment we wake up each day to the moment we enter the inner sanctum of our counseling office and begin our work. On a good day, we can compartmentalize and get on with our day. And then, there are **those** days...

No matter what your circumstances are-- married with or without children, or single with or without a significant other or children-- what happens to you before you get to school can often set the tone for your day. Mornings are a prime time for us to create our baggage for the day. It can range in the spectrum from the short-lived irritation, such as you got caught in traffic, to the "I'm soooo mad-- wait 'til I get home" irritation because you had an argument with a family member which didn't get resolved before you left. If you have never had this happen, I envy you because you truly do live a charmed life.

Granted, almost everyone brings a little bit of home with them to their workplace everyday, no matter what the job. However, in the case of a school counselor who must, on top of this, deal with what may have happened to someone else, such as a child or parent before they got to school that day, it can have its really tough moments, especially when we are emotionally charged ourselves. There is no easy answer to solving this dilemma. It all lies within the purview of your own coping skills, and cope you must.

In my own case, it was not a natural but a learned response. I did over the years get better and better at compartmentalizing my own feelings when I was concurrently dealing with a daunting issue at home and an emotional issue with someone else in my office, but I never found a solution that worked every time.

To pretend that there aren't going to be times when how you respond to someone you are counseling at school will be directly influenced by some emotional turmoil that you may be struggling with from home is to be in complete denial. We cannot separate who we are from what we do. If we could do that, we would all be androids, not humans. Let's get real. If you left your own child at home whining because he didn't get his way, you probably aren't going to feel overly compassionate that day when a kid shows up in your office whining about not getting her way. It's just plain difficult to stay objective every second of your life.

So, what do you do? The truth is, I don't have a ready answer. All I know is that you must get a handle on whatever is irritating you—catch yourself---before you see the first counselee, or you will be doing that child a disservice. You have to find what works for you. In some ways, it is rather ironic that we counsel kids not to push their feelings way down inside, and then we find that we have to suppress our own in order to cope with our day and hopefully be successful with helping others. It doesn't seem quite fair, but it comes with the job.

I will say one thing. I did get better with practice over the years because I had plenty of it. This is because you will find that it isn't just learning to compart-mentalize whatever personal issues that may be going on at home from those in your job. It is also trying to separate and maintain your objectivity when dealing with the emotional issue of the child who just left your office, and the next child who just came through the door. Your emotional response to one child has the potential to spill over to the next child, depending on how you, yourself, feel that day or how you feel about that child. It's a hard truth, but it has to be said, and believe me, you will get plenty of practice.

Since you must find your own way to separate your personal baggage of the day from the issues of those who come to you for help, my only suggestion is for you to become very aware of your own personality construct, that part of you that houses your *emotional self*. Work on expanding those coping skills that you have already acquired and successfully developed during your lifetime to include your *counselor self*. Otherwise, you may not be able to maintain personal emotional control and objective distance from the counselee who needs your assistance. If necessary, delay decisions until you are emotionally in a better place, unless the child is at-risk. If you doubt your objectivity, always be willing to consult a colleague.

Experience will be your inevitable teacher, and although you can never leave all of your worries on the doorstep before you leave home each day, you can get a handle on how you respond to a personal situation. Through effort on your part, self-awareness (catching yourself), and just plain necessity, you will strengthen your own coping skills and leave a lot more of your personal issues at home, which is exactly where they belong.

Chapter 7: Be a Human Being First

"The main thing in life is not to be afraid to be human."

Pablo Casals,
Conductor and Cellist

When I was in college in the early '70's, I had a poster on my dorm wall stating the Pablo Casals quotation above. It was always one of my favorites. I still have it packed away in a trunk somewhere, but it is still branded in my memory after all of these years.

You may wonder why I chose such a philosophical topic for a chapter in a book for counselors, but it seems quite appropriate to me because of the human problems that we have to deal with everyday. Although everyone is unique in their own way—physically, mentally, emotionally, and spiritually—we all share one common denominator: being human beings.

All of us bring to each day a culmination of who we are, what we have experienced, and the potential for who we will become. Each human being carries within him all of his hopes, dreams, and aspirations, as well as his fears, disappointments, and hurts. Although we as counselors may not access these feelings on a conscious level, they are always there and affect us when we are working with other human beings, whether they are children or adults. These qualities of being human connect us with all other human beings and can have either a subtle or perhaps not so subtle influence on how we deal with and respond to others. This is why it is important that we think about this topic.

As the saying goes, we can't un-ring a bell. We have to be who we are. Although objectivity is the number one goal in our profession if we are to help others help themselves, it is not so easy. To ask ourselves not to react as human beings when we deal with emotional issues is a tall order and one that we have to learn to defer until the child or parent has left our office.

There were times when I had to leave my office and go somewhere where I could be alone for a moment and allow myself to take a deep breath or even silently cry. I just couldn't hold on to the pain of another human being for one second longer, particularly a child's. If I hadn't taken the time to *depressurize* by having a moment alone or maybe taking a walk around the school to calm my anger or sorrow or sometimes frustration, I might not have been able to salvage the day. There were days when I could handle the pain and desperation of others and then other days when my emotions slipped through the web of my objectivity. Either way, I had to create my own personal survival skill for the benefit of the next counselee who would be entering my office.

Whether you like it or not, you will always be a human being first, and that's as it should be. It is being human that gives you as a counselor the ability to connect to and understand other human beings. Don't expect to become the Rock of Gibraltar, even if you work as a counselor for thirty years. However, you will have to learn to control your emotions in front of others in order to be effective in this job. Otherwise, you could become an emotional basket case, and for the sake of yourself and others, you would do well to look for another profession.

There will be times when your humanness will shine through your objectivity, and that's okay. It will show your counselees just how much you truly care. Don't be afraid to be human. Guard you heart, but always keep it open.

Chapter 8: Who are You Doing this Job For? There is No Place for Ego

"Experience is the name that everyone gives to their mistakes."

Oscar Wilde
Author, Playwright, and
Poet

Have you ever been trapped into a conversation with an egotistical person? Now, be honest. You know that you have to be polite. Nevertheless, behind that smile that you project while you fain interest in his self-important conversation hides a mouth full of clenched teeth and your not too admirable desire to either shake him silly or just escape. An egotist is a person addicted to himself, and although it is sad, really, it can certainly be hard to bear.

But now let's look at egotism in a different way. Some people will argue that we all have to possess a certain amount of ego to have enough confidence to do our job. Otherwise, we would be viewed as insecure and project inadequacy. From that perspective, I would say that this is a reasonable statement. Perhaps the concept of ego should be looked at not as a single trait, but according to degrees.

So, where does ego fit into your job as a school counselor? Should it fit at all? You will need to dissect this issue for yourself. Do you need some ego and a strong concept of self to be an effective counselor? I would say, yes. Should you be so confident that you think that your way is always the best way, and you don't need anyone else's suggestions on how to deal with an issue? That would be overconfidence, and, of course, experience will teach you otherwise. Ego and arrogance are twins, and no matter how open-minded that you may think you are, all of us will at times believe that we are right and everyone else is wrong. Maybe in some cases we are right, but how will you know if you don't listen to others and have a frame of comparison? Any idea can look good when it stands alone, but it may show hidden weaknesses when compared to another.

I am by no means trying to say that you should always make a comparison with every idea that you devise. I am just saying that if you are so determined to have your own way that you have no trouble shutting out every other person's ideas, you may be creating a potential problem. Take a moment to look left and then right because ego and arrogance are probably sitting on both sides of you at the table, and your mind is beginning to narrow. Deep emotion is a good barometer for signaling that you may be losing perspective. Emotion begins to beat up logic, and then ego lifts its ugly head and mistakes happen because your vision gets clouded. This can cause even a good idea to fall by the wayside that could with a little tweaking have worked. The experience and ideas of your fellow school counselors can be not only beneficial but a good barometer for testing your own objectivity. Always be open to consultation.

I may sound like I am trying to kill your enthusiasm, but I am not. It's just a good idea to remind yourself now and then about who you are doing this job for. Is it to build your own ego and look good to others, or is it to make the life of someone else better? This is not an insulting remark. It is a realistic one. All of us want to do things in our life that help us to feel good about ourselves and to feel a sense of accomplishment. Otherwise, our spirit would languish. However, as a counselor, this should not be our driving force. You are there to do a job, and your job is to do what you can to help other people during difficult times in their lives. You have to be willing to find the best way to do this, and this will not necessarily be your way all of the time. Sharing your thoughts with others and allowing them to reciprocate will give depth and more substance to your ideas, since they will be nourished by the positive and negative experiences of others. This will be beneficial for the person you are seeking to help, and for yourself, because you are more likely to make less errors in judgment that you will be berating yourself for later.

As my colleague Roxanne says about counseling, it's like using Elmer's glue: apply white, hold everything together, but with the finished product the glue will be transparent. A counselor's best work is when the student, parent, or staff member has solved her own problem with your guidance. You are there to help that person build her own solving skills.

Don't deny that you have a certain amount of ego, but if you find that you just have to prove that you are right and everyone else is wrong, just remember that egotist who caused you to clench your teeth may be smiling back at you.

Chapter 9: The Desire to Control Can Choke You

"I claim not to have controlled events, but confess plainly that events have controlled me."

> Abraham Lincoln
> Letter to A. G. Hodges,
> [April 4, 1864]

Are you what we euphemistically call a *Control Freak*? It doesn't sound like a very counselor-like question, but I am asking you this question again in the current and not-so-kind vernacular: Are you a control freak? Although you may find this question a little insensitive on my part (remember I warned you earlier that you may not always agree with me), it is probably one of the most important questions that you need to ask yourself at the beginning of your counseling career. How you answer it, if you can be completely honest with yourself, will give you insight into how you are likely to handle the day-to-day stresses of your job and whether or not you might *burn out* early.

There is nothing necessarily profound in your answer. All of us as human beings suffer under the delusion that we have control over our lives. Perhaps nature imprinted it in our DNA as a survival skill so that we aren't afraid of everything and everyone. Just a thought--there is no evidence to support this idea. I am sure that it is just a rationalization on my part—the part of me that would like to think that I have at least a little control over the forces of life, or is it just my left brain trying to reassure me? Who was it that said, "Man plans, God laughs?" (an old Yiddish proverb).

I wouldn't be so bold as to say that all counselors tend to be controllers because that certainly is not true. However, counselors, by the nature of their work, do have to keep a lot of things under control so that they can successfully accomplish their job (multi-tasking, making quick transitions, and compart-mentalizing). The landscape around you can, and often will, change moment to moment and day by day. Kids, parents, teachers, and others will show up when they are feeling out of control. It will often fall to you to get an out-of-control person under control, while keeping your own emotions in balance. You will also be expected to keep your work load, interpersonal relationships with your colleagues, as well as administrative expectations, county expectations, family concerns, and your own expectations of yourself under some semblance of control, too. Ah, juggle those balls in the air. The pressure is on!

Putting all of this aside, we have to backtrack to the original question again because being able to control the situations that you are confronted with everyday in a professional way and being a *controller* are really not the same thing. One may impact the other, but they are still different. How you handle your own emotions as you deal with one frustration after another, one consequence after another, one less-than-hoped-for outcome after another will clue you in to just how much of a controller that you really are.

Your own nature, your family dynamics currently and while you were growing up, your attitude towards life, and your expectations of yourself and others have all contributed to molding your sense of who you are and how you view yourself in relation to the world. So ask yourself the following question: What is the world to you? Is it a place of untold and exciting possibilities, or is a place where you must be on guard twenty-four/seven because the world is an unpredictable and scary place, and you must be prepared for whatever could be waiting just around the next corner to pounce on you? Can you live with the uncertainty?

I am not attempting to psychoanalyze you, nor am I asking you to do it yourself. However, your perception of yourself and of the world will influence whether or not you will constantly try to force your own will on others in an attempt to control the ever-changing and ever-challenging slippery slope of your job and your life. If you find yourself trying to control every situation and the outcome to every decision that you make in your career and discover that you become frustrated or angry with yourself and others when things don't go as planned, then you are a controller.

It may be an oxymoron but it's true: *you need to get the controller in you under control.* If you don't, I can promise you that you will always be surrounded by doubt. Nothing that you do will ever be good enough, and you will become miserable both inside and outside of school because you will constantly be judging yourself by a measuring stick that you can never live up to. Furthermore, and I know that this is going to sound brutal, it is bad enough that you choose to do this to yourself by what I believe to be a lack of self-awareness more than blind intention, but it is totally unfair to make the other people around you suffer your negative reactions. I say this with compassion because I know what it is to have control issues, so I certainly can't cast a stone at you from my own glass house.

In reality, no matter how hard we human beings try, we will always bring who we are to our job, but, in the case of a counselor, who we are and our personal perceptions can affect how we influence those who we are attempting to help. You must be self-aware as a matter of ethics because you have a moral obligation to those who you will be working with, and you must catch yourself if you discern that you are trying either voluntarily or involuntarily to interject your own control issues into the guidance that you are sincerely trying to give to others. No one is perfect, so understand that you will not be able to catch yourself all of the time. Just keep working on your self-awareness from the first day to the last day of your career, and try to carry it over into your personal life for the sake of yourself and others.

Whether we can ever change our personality or our ingrained perceptions is highly debatable and really a moot point. We have to deal with what is and what brought us to this moment in time, and if we are a controller, either by nature or nurture, we have to make a conscious effort to distance ourselves from that part of us that can prejudice the support and information that we freely give to others. If we don't, then we have compromised our objectivity, which can backfire on us, should we find ourselves giving advice and not options to others. Trying to force unreal expectations on ourselves and other people can lead us to both physical and emotional burn out, even though our efforts to help others are both strong and sincere.

Chapter 10: Teaching and Teachers: Same Song, Different Verse

"School counselors are teachers with a different lesson plan."

> Robin Di Peppe
> Retired School Counselor
> and Teacher

Contrary to popular belief, school counselors and teachers are not natural adversaries. I can realistically speak to this fact having been both. Yes, there will always be some naysayers who think that all we do is sit around drinking coffee, yakking, and dealing with kids and parents at our own leisure. Of course, there are people from all walks of life who can be lazy and don't do their job justice. School counselors are no exception, but we counselors really have been unfairly labeled as a profession for a long time. It can be quite aggravating, but it unfortunately comes with the terrain. It is up to you to dispel the myth.

Even people from counseling backgrounds can buy into this preconceived notion of the role and mentality of counselors. As an example, many years ago I was actually told by someone in the school counseling field to always carry a briefcase to and from work, so that teachers would see that counselors take work home, too, and might not be so resentful of us. Personally, I always found that this suggestion propagates the myth that we don't work as hard, and it is also an insult to teachers. If you want to carry a briefcase or shoulder bag, that's great (I did), but carry it for yourself and not because you feel that you have to justify your job or impress someone else.

It is a fact that there will be some teachers who will constantly be on the defensive because they will assume that talking to a school counselor is a big waste of time. Why? Because they have prejudged us as a bunch of bleeding hearts who will automatically take the side of the child and create excuses for him, rather than hold him accountable for his actions. Some administrators will hold this same opinion of counselors, too, and will only bring you into a situation at the request of the parent or child or when a child refuses to talk or gets too emotional for them to deal with. Expect that this will probably happen.

The good news is that in my experience, these judgmental teachers are in a very small minority and are easy to identify. They will be the ones who will rarely, and unexpectedly, show up at your door and be absolutely irate as they inform you that they have had it with some child and/or his parent. This teacher has probably done everything that she can think of first and has just had enough, or she wouldn't have come to see you as a last resort. You may not be able to get in a word edgewise until she has finished telling you what "Little Lucifer" did to destroy her class that day (and everyday). Another probable scenario is that she has taken all of the verbal abuse that she is going to take from a rude and unreasonable parent, so now you can be the one to deal with this situation.

Try not to prejudge these teachers as they may have prejudged you. If you were a classroom teacher before you became a counselor, you know exactly what I mean. Teachers have feelings and breaking points, too, even the experienced ones. Sometimes civility doesn't make any impact on an angry and irrational parent, so it is appropriate for the teacher to defer the problem to the counselor, rather than sink to the level of unprofessionalism.

Teachers work extremely hard and can be greatly under-appreciated for the important work they do. Sadly, you may be under-appreciated, too. Sometimes they just need to come to your office to vent from sheer frustration and exhaustion. Give them a safe and nonjudgmental place to do that, whether that particular teacher truly appreciates what you do or not.

In defense of any teacher, the bottom line is this: one child should not be allowed to ruin the education of a whole class, and this is where you as a counselor come into play. You may not be a miracle worker, but part of your job is to help the child get himself together so the teacher can do her job for the benefit of everyone. If you are successful, an administrator may not have to intervene and bring in that rude and unreasonable parent, who thinks the school is picking on her child, for a parent conference from hell.

Don't misunderstand this statement. I do not mean to sound harsh. The child and possibly the parent are clearly in need of some kind of help, even if the child is just a proverbial chatterbox and not a child who is completely out of control. Either way, something has to be done for the sakes of the teacher and the other students. By the act of this teacher angrily appearing at your door, you have now identified another child who you need to work with, probably on an ongoing basis. Attitudes can be difficult to change, but being supportive of the teacher by listening and making a good faith effort to help improve the situation, even in small increments, can begin to change the perspective of even the most judgmental teacher.

Looking at the big picture, having spent my tenure equally divided behind both desks, I can tell you that the jobs of teaching and school counseling have more similarities than they do differences. Think about it. Teachers have a classroom, and you have an office and, hopefully, a conference room for your teaching. They have a class roll, and you have a case load. They have a curriculum for their subject area, and you have your federal, state, county, and school standards, mandates, and individual goals. They make lesson plans, and so do you. In most school systems you will do classroom presentations, as well as small group work on various issues (self-esteem, study skills, bullying, grief, anger management, testing, etc.), and in reality, you will create a mini-lesson plan for every child who comes into your office with an problem.

Sometimes you will be able to use a lesson plan that you have already created because the child's issue is the same one, or similar to, an issue that you have dealt with many times, either with the same child or a different child. You just may have to adjust it a bit each time you reuse it, that's all. Then again, you may be confronted with a totally new issue, and you will have to use all of your knowledge and experience to create a new lesson plan that fits this new situation. It may end up being a plan that is a "one hit wonder" and solves the problem immediately, or you may have to create a lesson plan that will expand over time as you work with an individual child or perhaps another child with the same issue.

In the final analysis, it really is no different than what a teacher does. When teachers get asked a question out of left field (kids tend to think that teachers are supposed to be a walking encyclopedia about everything --at least, some of mine did!) or perhaps look out at a bunch of blank faces of students who just aren't getting it, they also have to think fast on their feet and differentiate their instruction in an effort to communicate a concept to a particular class or group of individuals. This is how we all create and collect strategies and methods that will work. Over time we learn which ones work and which ones don't.

As a school counselor, you will need to make a concerted effort to become part of the team. If you don't want to be viewed as the orphan child of the building (neither teacher nor administrator), then it is up to you to define your role. You can't do this from your office. You need to be seen all over the building, not just at mandatory faculty meetings. Paula, one of my directors, stressed that counselors need to make themselves visible on the bus ramp, in the halls, and in the cafeteria as often as possible, as well as touch base with each counselee during the first month of school, so they will know that you are there for them. It may be a time-consuming task, but it will be worth your effort.

Teachers can't leave their classrooms, so if there is a problem, you go to them in between classes. Not only meet with individual teachers, ask if you can attend one of their teacher or grade-level meetings. Get to know them as a department and LISTEN TO THEM. Let them vent their frustrations and concerns as individuals and as a group. Even if you can't solve all of their concerns, you might be able to solve some. You can also learn a lot about what is going on in the whole school setting by listening to those who are also "in the trenches" everyday. I know that you are busy, but it is crucial that you make the time to do this. The kids and administrators need to see this, too. You are an integral part of school life. Don't let them perceive you as a spider hanging in a corner.

When I was assigned a grade level at one of my schools, I used to begin the school year by asking the teachers during their planning week to give me a time that was convenient _for them_, and I would bring cookies or candy, and we would talk about their concerns and what they wanted me to help them with that year. Point blank asking the question, "What do **you** need me to do to help you this year, and are there any areas that you would prefer to handle as a grade level or department without my intervening?" is the first step in bridging the perceived gap between you and your teaching colleagues. It puts you on equal par with them, which is exactly where you should be.

Most teachers are quite capable of handling their own problems. Don't stomp on their turf. You are there as part of their support system, not to dictate. When they need you, they will let you know, and they should be part of the solution. They deserve that respect. Only circumvent a teacher if you perceive that she may have lost all objectivity. That can happen to any of us. Otherwise, teamwork with teachers, administrators, staff, and parents should be "a given" in your effort to help a child. Collaboration is an essential counselor skill.

Chapter 11: Don't Break the Rules, but…: Walking a Fine Line

"The Power belongs to him who knows,"…"and he who knows is then responsible."

Sanscrit and Eden Gray,
<u>The Complete Guide to the
Tarot</u>

Sounds a little suspicious—'Don't Break the Rules, but…" It's the word "but" that might make you wonder if I was a maverick counselor. I really wasn't. There were times when I got a little creative, but I didn't break the rules. Rules are there for a reason. Make sure that you understand what they mean. Rules can be left open to interpretation if they are not clearly stated, and different interpretations can lead to all kinds of trouble.

In graduate school you have or will study counselor rules and ethics. Most likely you will be directed towards the <u>Ethical Standards for School Counselors</u> set by the American School Counselor Association (ASCA). I always looked to the ASCA National Model for clearly defined regulations that should be followed by professional school counselors. If you haven't read them yet, I suggest that you do so every year. New dilemmas may modify or create new guidelines. These standards are very explicit and make clear where you should draw the line in your decision-making. Discuss them with your colleagues. You will also need to know your state and county/city laws, as well, because these can be changed, also.

So, why did I say, "Walking a Fine Line?" Because in any given circumstance that we encounter during our career, it is difficult sometimes to neatly fit a particular scenario into one of these well-defined rules. There are a thousand variations on a theme and even a minor difference between one child's situation and another's may have you questioning whether or not a particular rule or regulation applies to him.

Beyond the obvious ones like "Duty to Warn" or reporting abuse or neglect, it can be disheartening to work with a situation that needs attention but may place you in a position where someone could question if your involvement has become too personal, or whether or not you should have become involved at all. Sometimes walking that "fine line" can become a judgment call, and the call may not in the end be decided by you.

Look at the following example and see the tangle that could arise:

ASCA Ethical Standard A- 4 states the following:

> *Avoid dual relationships that might impair his/her objectivity*
> *and increase the risk of harm to the student (e.g., counseling*
> *one's family members, close family friends, or associates). If*
> *a dual relationship is unavoidable, the counselor is responsible*
> *for taking action to eliminate or reduce the potential for harm.*
> *Such safeguards might include informed consent, consultation,*
> *supervision, or documentation.*

Suppose you are your counselee's Sunday school teacher, and you socialize with the child's parents. This is a *dual relationship*. The standard says "avoid," which is not an absolute *no*. Both the child and parents want you to be their school counselor, but you have to ask yourself whether or not you can really be objective in this situation. This is not an easy decision.

Putting aside the *dual relationship*, suppose a parent comes to you asking for help for her out-of-control child. She then informs you about situations or problems at home that are not connected to school. You may see how this can influence the child, but counseling the parent on non-school related issues is crossing the line into therapy. Be careful. Counseling must be school-related.

In many ways, school counselors can often walk a fine line. Everyone has his own perspective in any given situation. For example, when you listen to both sides of a story involving a parent and child, you may wonder if either or both are telling the truth or bending the facts to validate their own position. Kids and parents can both out-and-out lie. If so, am I helping the parent to create wrong strategies for the child? Have I given the child ideas on how to cope based on wrong information? Will I lose the child's trust if the parent has asked me to keep her office visit confidential, but the child finds out because his best friend saw his mom leaving my office? Will the child then think that I am going to take the parent's side? Should I suggest that the mom and child meet with me together to sort out what is going on? All of these are possible scenarios.

Perhaps your mind doesn't work like mine. However, in my defense, I learned over the years to be circumspect in my dealings with both parents and children when they both sought my help. As I said earlier, not every situation is black and white. They are often gray, and it is in that gray area that I felt uncomfortable sometimes. You may think that I am making a bigger deal out of this than I should, but honestly, there were times when I felt that I was really walking a fine line when dealing with the interpersonal relationships of my students. I always relied on my understanding of counselor ethics and tried to keep as objective as possible. However, you may find out, as I did, that it is easy to skate too close to that ethical boundary, even when you mean well. Once words are said in a conversation, you can never take them back.

I am not trying to make you paranoid about every word you say. That's a sure way to make you tongue-tied. What I suggest is that you know your ethics and all local, state, and federal regulations, and if you have any doubt about where the line is drawn in any situation, put off the conference and speak to your director, supervisor, or principal before you take on a situation that is questionable.

One time I actually excused myself from a conference for a minute while a parent was sitting in my office because I wasn't sure if I should be meeting with that person at all. I quickly pulled the student file, spoke with the principal who knew about the situation, and he intervened and spoke to the parent, as well. You would be surprised how your good intentions can be manipulated against you by some shrewd and dishonest people.

If you become concerned that you may have been caught up in a situation that could have legal or ethical repercussions, talk immediately to your director and principal and bring them on board. This is unlikely to happen when you know the law, but I always feel that it is better to be safe than sorry. You also may want to think about investing in some kind of Tort Insurance, which many teachers and counselors do, so that you are protected against law suits. It is inexpensive, and I never had to use mine, but it is a great safety net because we can never depend on the perception or stability of anyone who walks into our office.

Chapter 12: Learning to Do Triage and Damage Control

"Surgeons must be very careful,
When they take the knife.
Underneath their fine incisions
Stirs the Culprit—Life!"

Emily Dickinson
"No. 108," 1859

I was in college when the TV series *Mash* first made its appearance on the small screen. It was there that I learned what the word *triage* means. In general terms, *triage* means, "sorting out." In medical terms, it means, "a process of sorting patients according to urgency of illness or injury, in order to ascertain in which order to treat them in (Wiktionary, online). In counselor terms, it means to evaluate, classify, and prioritize your counselees according to the seriousness, urgency, or necessity of handling a present, pre-existing, or ongoing situation (my definition). By the time I retired, I felt that *triage* had become my middle name.

In general terms, I used triage to sort out the order in which I would see my counselees at any given time. It was not unusual for me to receive six to ten request slips from students per day. When I had that many (or more), I would do triage by dividing them into two groups according to the reason for the request. I saw those marked *Personal* first. In many cases, it was a child whose feelings had gotten hurt or thought that she had been treated unfairly, but, on the other hand, it can be shocking how kids can sit on a very serious problem for some time and not let anyone know. I had kids who were abused, pregnant, stalked, or suicidal come out of nowhere, and it could be chilling. The difference of one day can be scary.

Try to see your personal requests everyday, if you can. You are not responsible for what happens, and sometimes you just can't get to them all because an issue with one student can take up most of your day (example, abuse, having to bring in Social Services), but always try. If you are tied up and are worried about a child with an at-risk history, ask a fellow counselor to check in with the student and evaluate how serious the problem may be. Sometimes it is the best that you can do at that moment because there will be days when multiple serious issues can attack you at once. *Academic* requests can usually wait a day, if necessary. Always err on the side of caution, and don't be reticent to ask for help when you are confronted with more than one serious situation.

In a broader sense, I often felt like all that I was capable of doing was triage in some situations. So many of the issues that were brought to my office were after the fact or perhaps sometimes ongoing. That was when I had to do *damage control*. The fight in the hall had already happened, the child had already cursed at the teacher, the child and parent had already had a hurtful verbal battle that morning before the child came to school, the parents are divorced and use the child as a pawn against one another on a continuing basis, or the child was abused and under the auspices of Social Services already. In all cases, the damage has already been done before the problem gets to you.

Unfortunately, these are common occurrences, and a counselor can sometimes feel that all of her efforts are no more than putting a band-aid on a major wound. None of these situations can be undone, and some of them can only be healed with expert help. All you can do is use triage and decide which situations you are qualified to handle and which ones need to be passed on to another resource. You cannot be all things to all people, and both parents and students can sometimes look to you to wave a magic wand and be the great fixer of all things. This is not what you are there for. Your job has limitations and to go beyond them puts you in the unenviable position of being brought to task or sued for infringing on counselor ethics or the law. Counselors have lost their jobs for stepping beyond their qualifications, even though they meant well. Good intentions will not save you. Forgetting that you are a school counselor and not a therapist can torpedo your career in a flash and may cause irreparable damage to a child. It has happened and has been well-documented in numerous counselor journals.

The answer to all of this is to know your boundaries, do damage control when the issues are school-related, seek advice from school officials if you are unsure, and keep a list of multiple resources in your desk drawer so that you know who to contact if needed. Also, document your efforts in critical cases that may take you close to legal or ethical edges. Above all, strive to stay objective because many situations cannot be repaired by you, and it can be depressing. We cannot save people, but we can educate them about available resources and options and attempt to direct them onto a path where they can make positive decisions in their life.

Chapter 13: Pressure and Time Management: Beware of the "Quick Fix" by Active Listening, Guided Questioning, and Prioritizing

"He knew the precise psychological moment when to say nothing."

Oscar Wilde,
The Picture of Dorian Gray

The title of this chapter may seem to be ridiculously obvious for a counselor, but time used unwisely can become your nemesis. When I look back at my counseling skills, especially when they were being tested under pressure, I have to plead guilty to sometimes rushing to a conclusion and speaking when I should have kept my mouth closed a little bit longer. I was listening, but I let my own ongoing thought processes push me to suddenly interject a question or state-ment into the conversation that would later prove to be either irrelevant or unnecessary. Why? Because I let the pressure of time constraints get to me, and I talked too soon when I should have listened more. Inevitably, I would have to back up, reevaluate, and correct my thinking. My consequence would then be in direct correlation to the time that I had wasted. Therefore, I had to use more time than I would have to find a possible solution than if I had controlled my impulse to speak.

My error, of course, was giving in to pressure and not having listened to the whole story first. I assumed that I had an easy answer for the problem, often-times because I had heard the same story so many times before. In my head I had created a *quick fix* and had filled in the gaps of the story with what I *thought* that it was all about. Done. Now move on to the other counselees waiting impatiently outside of my office and an administrator who is standing at my door.

It is this kind of pressure that can force counselors to super glue a situation together without having all of the pieces, so that we can move on to the next possible dragon at the door. However, it is also a great disservice to the child who is sitting in the chair across from you. That child was there first, and his issue is just as important to him as someone else's is to her. He deserves the necessary time to work out his problem. He also deserves to be heard completely so that you are sure that you have an accurate picture of what is really going on.

Situations may be similar, but again we need to remember that each child brings his own personality and perspective to what is happening, so we need to gauge our responses accordingly. Therefore, there really should never be a quick fix no matter what the circumstances are or how many people are waiting for you. That would be assuming that every person or situation is exactly alike, and we know that's not true. People are similar but not clones.

As Lenny, one of my colleagues and the supervisor of my internship, once said, "You want to treat your counselees in the way that you would want someone to treat your own child." I totally agree. Don't rush through a situation for expediency. That would be cheating the child.

But what do you do when so many things conspire against you and all at the same time? Suppose you have a kid in your office who is rambling on and on with no real direction, a fellow counselor who is sitting in the back room with one of your girls who dashed into the Counseling Office crying hysterically, and another two counselees who have been sent to you by teacher passes (teachers and administrators will sometimes send kids to you with no warning). Oh, yes, and the administrator is still there. How do you give this child in your office your full attention but move the situation forward?

Suddenly you feel like you are being torn in every direction. This child is here. Others are waiting, the child in the back room obviously needs your attention, and your fellow counselor and the administrator need to get back to their own office to deal with their own work load. Ah, also throw in the fact that your phone is now ringing (it will ring at least four times before your voicemail picks up), and your train of thought has just jumped the track. There were times when I felt as if my head were going to explode. If only there were a quick fix! Here are some strategies that may help, but you will need to create a strategy that works for you.

Hopefully by now the administrator has waved at you through the door and mouthed, "See me later" so that he can happily escape all of the emotional ruckus in the Counseling Office. He knows he can't win and probably has kids, teachers, or a parent waiting for him at his own office door. If not, motion to him that you will come to see him later. If it had been important enough, he probably would have interrupted you by now, anyway. So one in your waiting line has now gone (temporarily).

Now, back to the rambling kid in your office. It is time to *check in* to make sure that you are on the right track. "John, I want to take a moment to summarize what you have told me.....(summarize). Is this right?"

Now close off your inner voice and really *actively listen*. Let him add any missing parts while you keep him from straying off-topic. Hopefully, by guiding him to focus, you now have the necessary information to come to a solution. If not, you must now prioritize.

You may have to say to him, "John, I would like to consider some options for you. Let me think about this and have you come back to my office a little later today so we can decide what is best. In which class do you not have a quiz or test or is the easiest for you to make up the work if you miss a few minutes?"

Listen carefully to his answer. This small thing will add insight into your knowledge of the child. This is how you catch what I call the "skaters" who will use any reason to see their counselor so that they can skate out of class and have an excuse for not doing their work. ("Remember, Mr. Smith? I was with my counselor when you gave that assignment.") This is when you pull out his report card from the copies that you handily keep in your upper drawer. You can quickly discover if it is his best class or if he just wants to avoid a teacher or class that he doesn't like. Feel free to choose another class for him if you don't agree with his choice. Then remind him to ask his teacher what he missed and send him on his way. Make a note to call him back in so he doesn't get lost in your hectic day. So long as you call a child back in later, you won't have shorted him on the time he deserves. The next one in line is now gone (temporarily).

Concerning the hysterical child in the back room, one thing is for sure. You will learn over time which of your counselees are "drama queens," who will demand your attention every so often by pitching a fit, and which children are deeply suffering. Sometimes the kid in the back room may have to be the one who waits a little while if something more serious has just walked into your office. If she is a known "Drama Queen," stick your head in the door to let her know that you haven't forgotten her, make sure she has a box of tissues, and tell the counselor (if the child is no longer crying) that you know this student well and have great confidence in her ability to calm herself down while she waits for you. Assure the child that it won't be long. This releases your colleague to return to the children who now may be waiting for her while validating this child's feelings. Although drama queens can be quite trying, they have their own set of issues, too, and equally deserve your time.

Now briefly go to the kids who have been waiting impatiently at your door. Be frank with them. They probably saw and heard the child come into the office crying and watched your colleague take her into the back room.

"Fred, Alice… I want to spend time talking with each of you, but as you can see, I have a student who is really upset. Is this something that can wait until a little later today or even tomorrow when I can give you the time you need for me to listen and help?" Ninety-nine cases out of a hundred, the kids will say, albeit grudgingly, that they can wait.

Sometimes I found with high school kids that they would go up to the secretary and fill out an *Appointment Request*- bless them-before I even opened my door because they knew they didn't have a gnat's chance of seeing me anytime soon when a student came in crying. Most kids will be willing to wait and come back to see you later so that they can have your undivided attention.

Ask each student to fill out an *Appointment Request* and check whether it is for a *personal* or *academic* issue. Glance quickly at the request. If it is academic, give that student a pass to return to you later that day or tomorrow. I am not de-emphasizing academic issues, but as I said earlier, in these stressful times, err on the side of personal before academic.

If it is personal, take the child into your office and assess if it is an issue that can wait for later in the day or whether he should remain in the Counseling Office to talk to you. Look closely at his demeanor, tone of voice, and body language. The truth is that this child may have a more severe issue than the child who is railing in the back room. There are children who have learned to hide their desperation well.

So many times I found that the children with the most serious problems were not willing to reveal the real reason why they wanted to see you, especially after they realized that they wouldn't be able to meet with you right away. They would be dismissive and act like it was no big deal. This might be an opportunity lost for the child who has finally gotten up enough courage to talk to you about something serious in his life. Although you can't see inside his head, you can use your observation skills. Whether you ask this child to go back to class or to sit down and wait for you will be a judgment call. Either way, put the students' requests on your desk along with the first child's and re-prioritize.

Should a student who has been waiting defiantly refuse to reschedule when asked, have her quickly step into your office and ask for a brief synopsis of the problem. If it is something that can wait, give the student a pass to come back later and tell her that she *must* return to class until you have dealt with the issue of another student who came in before she did. She may leave unhappy, but she will just have to be patient and wait for her turn. Now, hopefully, you can get to the girl in the back room, at last.

There will be times when both children who are waiting will have a serious issue going on, and it becomes almost impossible to decide which one to deal with first. This is when counselors need to step forward and share their time with their colleagues for the benefit of the child. It should never be that this is *your* student or *my* student but *our* student. Expect it of one another, and do it freely for one another.

It is difficult to come to terms with the fact that no matter how hard we try, sometimes a child with a serious issue gets past us due to the sheer number of students in our case load. We can't read their minds, and we can only focus on one situation in any one given moment. All we can do is continuously sharpen our skills through active listening, using guided questioning, observing body language, and prioritizing (and sometimes re-prioritizing) according to the information that we are given. It is your best shot at keeping as many at-risk kids as possible away from that ever-looming crack in the pavement.

The reality is that *you are only one person*. The pressures on some days will be great. People will demand that everything be done now. In many cases, that will be impossible. When people gripe at you because everything didn't get finished in one day, don't have any problem reminding them that you are only one person, and there are just so many hours in a day. This is not an excuse for not getting everything done; it will often be an inevitability. Assure them that you will get to whatever they need as quickly as you can, and then make sure that you do.

Counselors can receive a lot of criticism for delaying too long or not following through on a request. Everyone thinks that their request is the most important. They probably have little or no clue what you have to contend with on a day to day basis. Don't let them get under your skin (easier said then done when you feel beat to death already). Keep a list, prioritize, and get back to the child or adult in a reasonable time, even if it is to let them know that you have not yet finished the task. At least they will know that you haven't forgotten them or decided that their issue is not important. Even if you get a negative reaction from them, you know that you are doing everything you can to meet all of the requests that have been made for you to complete. Don't let their anger push you to the point that you put yourself under even more stress. They will have to wait their turn like everyone else.

Some of the best advice I ever received was from my high school director Susan. When I would let too many details or unresolved situations overwhelm me, she would say, "Remember. Nobody's dying and nobody's bleeding." Then I would pull things back into perspective and keep working through my current list of things to do. That advice has even carried over into my private life because it is far too easy to become overwhelmed in any aspect of our life, and we need to remember that in our job, as well as our life outside of school, that we cannot be all things to all people.

Being a counselor is just as draining as it is rewarding. Trying to find a balance will be an ongoing and unavoidable challenge. Even if there is a definite office protocol, teachers, administrators, parents, and children will drop in un-announced. Life happens in spite of your planned appointments. Having a strategy that keeps you on an even keel, even when your plans get interrupted, will benefit both you and your counselees when the day just isn't long enough.

Time management is the ultimate key to your survival. Create a management system that will work for you. Eventually, everything *will* get done.

Chapter 14: Hold Your Heart in Your Nearest Pocket

"But I will wear my heart upon my sleeve
For daws to peck at."

William Shakespeare
<u>Othello</u> I, i, 64

Your heart—your biggest asset and your greatest enemy. It is most likely the true underlying reason why you chose counseling as a profession in the first place, even though you may be able to espouse many other reasons, too. The truth is that *heart* links to love, love links to compassion, compassion links to wanting to help, wanting to help links to making a difference, and making a difference is why you are there. There is just no getting around it. *Heart* is at the core of what you do. However, your heart will become your enemy if it is allowed to rise up and overwhelm your objectivity. Beware. In human nature, it is the more powerful of the two forces.

So, how will you use your heart? The answer to that is connected to your individual mindset and also your personality. You know yourself better than anyone. What is your emotional construct? Are you a person whose feelings can easily get hurt? Do you care too much about what other people think of you? Do you take even a small criticism so personally that you begin to doubt yourself and let it eat away at you? Can even small sorrows or joys bring you to tears? That's okay. It is who you are. However, be aware that if this is you, then by nature you are a person who wears her feelings on her sleeve.

Out of necessity, you will have to train yourself to manage these personality traits because they will constantly test you in your job as a counselor. It will be difficult, but it will be imperative that you create a control switch to harness your natural impulses. Otherwise, your objectivity will go right out the window in any given situation, and it will be hard to get it back. Once your mind has created an emotional tie with the person or situation that you are dealing with, becoming objective again will probably come back only when you have stepped over the line or made some kind of mistake. Then it will be blatantly obvious that you lost your objective focus, even though your heart meant well.

Now just in case those of you who are very sensitive might begin to envy those who seem to handle people and situations with rock-hard objectivity, remember that appearances can be deceiving. Again, I will ask a set of questions to these individuals, also. What does objectivity mean to you? Do you project a too-hard wall of objectivity? If so, why? Is this your true personality, or have the circumstances of your own life caused you to hide your emotions in the stronghold of an all-to-fragile and wounded heart?

I am not trying to be a therapist. You are who you are, and that's okay, too, but you may have something to be concerned about, as well. If you smother your heart to the point that your objectivity has lost its humanity, then you will only be half a counselor. And remember, the emotions that you suppress still live there. Dealing with so many children and adults in difficult and sometimes heart-rending situations will undoubtedly hit upon the emotions that you may be trying so hard to control. I certainly found that out myself, and when the emotion unexpectedly broke through the wall of my objectivity, it was much more extreme than it would have been if I were a person who had worn my emotions more openly than I did.

So, constantly seek *balance*. You will learn it by necessity and through self-awareness and experience. Be patient with yourself, but never stop striving for that sometimes elusive state of equilibrium, for your counselees' sakes, as well as your own. It will be one of your most important survival skills.

I have just talked about the two emotionally-skewed edges of the human personality. Most of us are combinations of both, and depending on what kind of day it is, we can swing from one extreme to the other. So many things can influence our emotions and mood before we even walk through our office door.

Suffice it to say, heart and objectivity will always be at war, so finding and trying to maintain a balance between the two can be a continuous challenge. My suggestion is to keep your heart, but put it in your nearest pocket for safekeeping. To wear it on your sleeve will expose your own vulnerability, as well as leave you open to the manipulation of others. However, don't zip the pocket so that you forget it's there. Let your heart shine forth in the sincerity that you project to others as you help them through a challenging time in their life.

Chapter 15: Don't "Fix" the Problem: Teaching Life and Coping Skills as the Foundation for Survival—Yours and Theirs

"To strive, to seek, to find, and not to yield."

Alfred, Lord Tennyson
Ulysses

I think one of the first misconceptions that I had to confront when I became a counselor was that I believed I was there to try to fix things—to solve as many problems as I could in an effort to help anyone and everyone who might cross my path. Although my heart was in the right place, it didn't take long for me to realize that my desire to become a "Miss Fix-It" was just as much of a personal issue as an idealistic one.

I don't think that any of us counselors would deny that at least part of the reason why we chose this profession was to try to make things better and to bring some kind of sense to our own little corner of this chaotic world. Whether it is to soothe a crying child, help a frustrated parent, give support to an overworked teacher, or stomp on injustice whenever we see it, the desire to fix what is broken may just be an integral part of who we are and what gives us purpose in our chosen career.

But is trying to fix what is wrong the core of what drives us to do what we do, or is it something even deeper? The truth is, when we heal others, we heal ourselves. When we give hope to others, we give hope to ourselves. Emotions will interconnect. Could this be a symbiotic relationship that we could not perceive until we became a counselor? Judge for yourself.

Don't misunderstand what I am saying. I don't doubt anyone's sincerity in wanting to help others. I never doubted my own, but it is imperative that we separate the desire to fix a problem, which is a personal issue (often a control issue), from the desire to teach others how to fix their own problems, which is a life skill. However, learning this in graduate school is one thing. Implementing it in your career is another. The two ideas can become blurred.

As a counselor you can temporarily fix an issue and make it disappear for awhile, but I promise you that it will only disappear temporarily. That issue, even if it takes on another form, will reappear with the same person at a later date if you haven't helped the child acquire the necessary skills to either solve it or learn to cope with whatever the problem may be.

Whether it is dealing with a bully, learning anger management, coping with a loss, or dealing with uncontrollable circumstances at home, teaching a child the skills to confront life's obstacles not as a victim, but as someone who knows what to do and where to find help in difficult situations will empower him. The lesson is that no one, no matter what age, has to be victimized by either a person or a situation. Perhaps if more people had learned this at a younger age, we wouldn't have so many adults who believe that they are trapped by their circumstances and won't seek help. Teaching *personal empowerment* and *non-victimization* will be some of the most important skills you will ever pass on to others. Teach these skills every chance you get, both in individual and classroom settings, as well as to a parent who seeks your help. This really is a gift that will keep on giving.

While we strive to empower others, we also empower ourselves. Whatever issues that you as an individual have faced, coped with, or overcome have helped to create who you are. However, in your job you must witness the hardships, losses, and sometimes tragic circumstances of your counselees and realize that there are some circumstances that you have no power to change. It is then that you must draw upon your own coping skills if you are going to stay objective with others and control your own pain---and you will feel pain and sometimes helplessness. It is part of the landscape of your job.

Because your heart must be open, this becomes a very daunting task but an imperative one for the children's emotional survival, as well as your own. Coping with another's pain, particularly when it is a child's, will be a life skill that you will have to teach yourself. You cannot carry everyone's pain with you, or you will lose your ability to see clearly and focus on the options that you may be able to offer them. It is a basic survival skill that each counselor must learn if you want to keep from emotionally burning out early in your career. I have known counselors who could not do this. They were intelligent people with the desire to help others, but they could not find a way to take a back step when it came to emotionally-charged or tragic situations, and they ended up leaving the profession. It was truly unfortunate, but to have stayed without the ability to emotionally handle their own feelings would have been personally destructive and created a stumbling block in their ability to counsel others.

Whether our success as a school counselor in controlling what can oftentimes be intense emotions depends on our own individual emotional construct that is embedded in our personality, or whether we can learn or modify the way we respond to the emotions of others is an open question. However, it is just one of the many questions that you will have to ask yourself as you progress in your profession, and only you will be able to find the answer that will decide the course of your career. Time and experience will tell, as well as allowing yourself to be open to self-exploration.

Chapter 16: Not Everyone Wants to be Helped— or Can Be : Dealing with Resistance

"Fancy thinking the Beast was something you could hunt and kill", said the Head. For a moment or two the forest and all the other dimly appreciated places echoed with the parody of laughter. "You knew, didn't you? I am part of you? Close, close, close! I am the reason why it's no go? Why things are what they are?"

William Golding
The Lord of the Flies (1954) Ch. 8

As human beings, I am not sure that it is possible to avoid using *resistance* as a protective mechanism. When we realize that a situation may bring about pain or fear as a consequence, most of us don't rush in where angels fear to tread. Even if we realize in the big picture that facing the proverbial dragon would be best for us (like going to the dentist), it is so easy to find reasons to put off dealing with any circumstance that we wish to sidestep.

Putting aside physical pain, finding a way to prevent emotional pain is just as strong a force, if not stronger. It has long been said that a physical wound can heal, but an emotional wound can leave a scar forever. Words once spoken can never be taken back, and they can undercut a child's feelings of trust.

In dealing with resistance, there are several things to keep in mind. First of all, you should expect a certain amount of resistance from a counselee, especially if a child has been sent to your office for some offense or concern and not chosen to come to talk to you by his own free will. To be required to go to talk with a counselor can be very intimidating to a student and will immediately put him on the defensive. I don't blame the child. I would probably feel the same way.

Likewise, parents can be resistant, too. If parents are informed by an administrator that they need to see the counselor because of issues with their child, they are likely to react in a similar fashion. They may feel that they are being backed into a corner. If they don't go, it will appear that they don't care about their child. If they do go, they may have to divulge certain personal information that they would rather keep private or are afraid that they may be judged as weak in their parenting skills. In addition, I discovered that some parents will view you as an authority figure, especially if they had a less-than-happy school experience themselves, and they can come in with a deep chip on their shoulder and be quite verbal about how they hated school, too.

Whenever I was confronted with a parent who displayed a negative or resistant attitude before she even entered my office, I would always spend some time trying to disarm her first. I can be chatty when I choose to be. In a situation like this, I wouldn't even broach the subject that the parent had come in to discuss until I had let her see me as just another person and not some ghost of an authority figure leaping out from her past trying to manipulate or judge her in some way. Here is an example of a typical conversation that I would have with a defensive parent in an attempt to lighten the atmosphere before we got started: "Mrs. Jones? Hi, I'm Robin Di Peppe, John's counselor. Come on in. Have a seat. I am really glad that you could come. As you can see from the pile on my desk, it has been one of those days. Sometimes there just aren't enough hours, you know? Let me have your coat. I guess it hasn't warmed up much outside."

Usually this would illicit some kind of response from the parent, and they would chat back. If not, I would sometimes add one or two more comments and then get to the point of their visit. "Well, let's talk about John. He really is a good kid. I think he's just frustrated right now..." ALWAYS, ALWAYS start off with something positive to say about the child. Don't ever forget that you are talking about that parent's child, and it is instinctual for someone to protect and defend her offspring, even if the kid is driving her crazy, too!

Now, I realize that some of you reading this will think that I just sounded like a ditz. I assure you that I didn't speak to the parent in a ditzy voice, and I always projected my sense of confidence because I took control of the initial conversation and let her know that between the two of us, we would come up with a game plan to help her child. I just didn't want to begin any parent conference with even a glimmer of what might be interpreted as an intimidating or condescending attitude. I always tried to lay down a constructive base to build upon first. I guess that I always tried to be *user-friendly,* for lack of a better description.

Some of you will think that any dealings with a parent should always be strictly business-like. That's okay. You do what you think is right and what works for you. I more often than not used that method, too (dressed with a genuine smile, of course), except when it was obvious that I was being confronted with angry resistance.

There is no right or wrong way here. I chose to break parent resistance by creating what I felt was an equal playing field by demonstrating that I was just one more person who cared about her child. It was also why I chose not to hang my Master's degree on the wall in my office. I was one of the few counselors that I knew who decided not to do this. I felt that it could potentially create a barrier with some people by projecting the erroneous impression that I was somehow above them or perhaps smarter. You could also argue that displaying your diploma might give some people a feeling of confidence in your ability. Both are good arguments. Instead, I chose to make my office very colorful with posters, pictures, children's work, knick-knacks, stuffed animals, and figurines. The logic behind this was that I wanted both kids and parents to see that I had created a child-friendly and happy environment. It was just another way that I tried to make someone feel comfortable and welcomed and hopefully put a kink in any resistance that they might have had. I honed the art of being formal within my informal office. You don't have to project a chilly personality or office to be taken seriously.

So, now, what to do when you have a resistant child-- there is no one-size-fits-all answer. How you decide to deal with a child's resistance will vary, according to the personality of the child and the circumstances of the situation. Obviously, the technique for dealing with a child and dealing with an adult is not usually the same, but there are exceptions. You can always decide to approach the subject in a straight-forward manner, fashioning your words to fit the age of the person while emphasizing that you are there to help. Sometimes this is all you will need to break through their resistance, whether it is a child or a parent.

Then there will be the other times when you are met with stone cold silence. Children can be very good at that. Sometimes it is sheer defiance, sometimes it is embarrassment, and sometimes it is real fear because they have been told by a parent that they had better never talk to a counselor. You may never know which of these scenarios might be causing the child to stonewall you. This is when you may need to find creative ways to break through the child's resistance. My suggestion is to let your own personality shine through and discover ways that work for you to gain that child's trust. Be patient.

If the resistant child is one you know because you have met with him before and gained some knowledge of his personality, you might use something akin to the following non-judgmental and non-intimidating statement to try to break the ice. Note: Counselors don't always have to start with an open question. Children often need reassurance to open up. "David, I get the feeling that you are having a tough day. How you acted in class doesn't seem to be the kid I know. I know you're upset and may not want to be here, but if you tell me what happened, we will work it out." (Silence) "Well, you can't go back to class while you are still upset, so why don't you sit here for a few minutes until you feel better and then if you want to talk, we will. If not, at least you won't carry your anger out of this office. It's better to leave it here in my office than ruin the rest of your day."

Giving the child a "cooling off" period or a safe place to vent if you can't break through is what you should strive for. Even if he won't talk, at least he will have time to get his feelings under control before he leaves. Don't ever let a child leave until you are confident that he can handle himself. Otherwise, he may become a discipline problem waiting to happen.

For a child who you may be meeting with for the first time, you might say, "Hi, "Mary. I am Mrs., Mr. Ms. _____, your counselor. Come in and sit down. Wow, take a deep breath. You look so angry. Don't worry. Whatever is going on, we can deal with it. That's why I'm here." Again, you are taking control of the situation while trying to reassure the child that everything is going to be all right and that you are not judging her. (Silence). "You know, Mary. Even if you feel that you are being treated unfairly, we can find a way to resolve it, but I can't do that unless you talk to me about what is going on. I am ready to listen when you are ready to talk. It will be okay." (Wait).

I personally found that if I approached an upset child in a calm and conversational tone, they were less likely to view me as just another authority figure, i.e., the enemy. Over time, you will discover what works for you while you create and collect variations on how to approach resistance as you observe the diverse personalities of your counselees.

If you really can't seem to get the child to open up, I sometimes found it helpful to approach the situation through the back door or *reverse psychology*. I would tell him what he was being accused of doing, and in many cases, the child would break his silence by getting mad enough to defend himself. Most children want to tell someone their side, especially if they think that the teacher is picking on them. You will hear this one a lot. Once their anger is diffused, you can get to the root of the matter and discuss what happened.

Whether or not you can get the child to acknowledge his part in what has occurred is sometimes a toss-up. That will depend on his maturity level or personality. What is truly important in the long run is to help the child become self-aware and discuss ways that he can avoid getting into this kind of situation again. Teaching is such a big part of counseling.

"So, David, what can you do to keep yourself out of this kind of situation again?" or "David, how do you think you might have handled this situation in a way that would have avoided you having a conflict with your teacher?" By allowing him to figure out what he can do not only empowers him, but by making him consider what happened, he is indirectly taking responsibility for at least part of what took place by coming up with a solution. This may be the only acknowledgment that you will get from him.

It is a totally different situation when someone has sent a child to you because she seems to be depressed, or there is a fear that the child is being abused in some way. The resistance and silence that can emanate from this child can be deafening. It will tug at your heartstrings and can scare you. The child's body language and lack of eye contact tells you that something is wrong. It may or may not be abuse. You can't be sure unless you can find a way to break her silence.

Never assume anything. I know that there is nothing more frustrating than feeling in your gut that something is happening to a child and not being able to prove it. Social workers will tell you that unless you can show them a physical mark on the child, there is nothing that they can legally do, and mental abuse can only be proven in rare instances.

In either case, if the child is depressed, you have a "Duty to Warn" situation, and you must call the parent that day with the teacher's and your own concerns for the child's state of mind. Over time, if you can build a relationship based on trust with the child, you may be able to break through her resistance and discover what the truth is. In the meantime, your phone call to the parents alerts them that the school is now aware that there may be a serious problem brewing with their child and that everyone will now be watching. This sends a strong warning signal to an abusive parent.

On the other hand, it opens a door of communication with a parent who may have been really worried about his child and didn't know where to turn. It is usually a win-win situation in either case, although in some cases the child doesn't want the parent called. He needs to understand that your not making the call is not an option. If I had to explain the law to a child, I did. I also reminded him that his teachers and I care, too, so we would have called anyway. I would tell him that I was sorry that he was angry, but I would rather that he be angry with me than his having to feel that he had to deal with an upsetting problem alone.

Kids can put up a good front, but the truth of the matter is that they don't want to admit when they can't handle a situation. High school students, in particular, love to act like they are old enough to make their own decisions, but they are really just beating their wings against their cage because their pride won't let them admit that they aren't quite ready to fly free on their own yet. They will resist being helped, but one of the saddest cases that I ever confronted was when a parent came into a conference and looked at her child and said, "I'm sorry for what he did, but I have given up on him. I don't care if he comes or goes. He's a ninth grader now. He's on his own." I then watched the child lower his head to hide a tear that was rolling down his cheek, and I wouldn't be truthful if I didn't say that every one of us in the parent/teacher conference, especially us who were mothers, wanted to leap across the table at this woman and shake some sense into her.

In the end, I think that it is important to understand that resistance comes in many guises and was formed for many reasons that we may never know about.

The main thing is that you keep on trying and keep on discovering ways to break though and help as many children and parents as you can, even though you may have to deal with your own frustration as you look for a crack in their wall.

Chapter 17: How to Handle Getting Used

"How cheerfully he seems to grin,
How neatly spreads his claws,
And welcomes little fishes in
With gently smiling jaws."

Lewis Carroll
Alice's Adventures in Wonderland

I have never met anyone who enjoyed getting used. I have met people who will set themselves up to get used because they like to play the "victim game" and covet the attention that they will garner, but that is a totally different issue.

Getting used may be a part of life, but it is particularly hard to swallow when you as a school counselor have put a lot of time, effort, and caring into helping someone, only to find that they lacked the sincerity that you gave so freely to them. That is one of the many reasons that getting used is so hard. Why? Because when you help people, you become vulnerable by opening up a part of yourself to them by caring, and they can gain access to your emotions, which can be positively or negatively impacted by how they respond back to you.

Think of the powerful emotions that can be evoked when you find out that someone you spent a lot of time and perhaps emotional energy on smiled in your face and then stabbed you in the back. Do I sound too harsh? Not where human feelings are concerned. You are no different than anyone else except how you personally choose to handle this kind of issue when it happens to you.

Of course, you will react according to your own emotional construct, but before you can decide on how you are going to handle what has happened, your emotions will probably have broken in line. They will always tend to jump in first before you can take that deep breath that you will need to calm down and not lose perspective. If they don't, you're one in a million.

So, how did I respond to getting used more times in my career than I choose to remember? It is a fair question. Well, the intensity of my response depended on how much time and emotion that I had invested in the person. Overall, I think that anger got the best of me first. Then, depending on the situation, I sometimes felt hurt and occasionally a sense of betrayal. Then my intellectual side would kick in to calm me down. I did ponder whether or not some people even knew what a moral center was, let alone had one, or how others can live with themselves when they can so guiltlessly use other people. This would include kids who were manipulative and had known exactly what they were doing (usually older kids, but not always), parents, teachers, administrators, and any other Tom, Dick, or Harry who had entered my office with a hidden agenda.

Next, my ego usually bullied its way to the surface so that it could whisper wickedly in my ear the thing that I hated the most to hear: I had been made a fool of by caring, or I must have been really stupid not to see what was going on. Then after spending a certain amount of time berating myself, I would come full-circle and get angry all over again. It was only when I had finally had enough of my self-indulgent "Pity Party" that I would finally be able to focus and decide how I was going to handle what had occurred. This was me—not a pretty sight but all too human. Now, what to do?

What you decide to do will, of course, vary according to the situation. However, I suggest that you live by this cardinal rule: NEVER LET THEM SEE YOU SWEAT, meaning you must be a professional first. It's one thing to quietly explode in your office or share your feelings with a colleague. You have to work through your feelings. However, it is a totally different thing to react inappropriately in the middle of the Counseling Office or in an unconstructive way to the person who used you. I know that you will be tempted, but you cannot say exactly what you are thinking because you won't be able to separate your emotions from your response.

This does not mean that you shouldn't hold people accountable for their actions when possible or let them know that you were put in an awkward situation because of what they did. Remember, it is not what you say but how you say it that can make all of the difference. You can use it as a learning experience, if only to send them a subtle but clear message that you won't be following them down that path again.

Inevitably, what is done is done, and you may not be able to correct or change the situation. The only thing that you will be able to control is yourself, and you must. Always take "the high road." This is what I taught my own children. Don't ever allow someone to drag you down to their level by reacting negatively because you want some kind of pay back. It won't work, and even if you are right, you will come out looking badly. Also, try not to take these situations home with you because your family doesn't deserve to be affected by the negativity.

If it is any consolation, try to remember that people (both kids and adults) use *manipulation* for many reasons. Some have a need to control because they usually feel powerless in other aspects of their life, some use it because it is ingrained in their psyche as a coping skill, some use it as a cover for low self-esteem, some are insecure and use it as a protective device if they feel threatened (the "I'll get you before you can get me" mindset), some want you to take on the risk in case the situation goes wrong (the Teflon Effect), some are selfish and just want what they want or are determined to win at all costs, and some are just plain bullies. I could go on and on, but I won't.

I wish that I could tell you that as you gain more experience as a counselor, you will finally be able to avoid getting used. I can't. The good news is that your learning curve will improve every time you fall into a trap, though. You won't be able to avoid them all, especially when you look through the eyes of your heart first. When it comes to heart vs. logic, the heart will always be the deal breaker.

Just remember why you are there and try to stay centered. In my experience I found that people who use others will eventually create their own downfall, anyway. I call this "the Boomerang Effect." What we send out, both positive and negative, always comes back to us eventually in one form or another. Need I say more?

Chapter 18: When They Resent You: Managing the Negative Responses of Others

"If everyone minded their own business," said The Dutchess in a hoarse growl, "the world would go around a deal faster than it does."

Lewis Carroll
Alice's Adventures in Wonderland

You might be surprised by the many and various directions from which resentment can fly at you unawares. There may be times when you feel as if you are playing a game of dodge ball and you are "It." Have you ever heard the old saying, "No good deed goes unpunished?" Even doing the right thing at the right moment will not always save you from the anger or possibly the resentment of someone else. Don't be surprised if your response towards other people's resentment of you is also resentment. Counselors have feelings, too.

I think that it is pretty safe to say that it is the nature of the beast for people to symbolically mark their territory and expect everyone else to respect their individual domain. An extreme example was the character Les Nessman, the quirky news reporter in the late 1970's sitcom *WKRP in Cincinnati*. He actually drew a square on the floor around his desk to mark the invisible walls and door to his office and demanded that people knock before they could enter. Likewise, there will be some individuals from both inside and outside the workplace who will put up invisible walls because they dislike the role you play and view you as an interfering busybody or, perhaps, an obstacle in their path. I never found this to happen on a large scale, but the times it did, I would have to sit in my office for awhile and get my irritation under control because of someone's mis-perception of my purpose.

Remember how the king in ancient lore used to kill *the messenger* with bad news? Well, guess what? Sometimes, you really are "It." There will be numerous circumstances when you get selected (or forced) into the position of being that messenger. This is when you will need to put on your cloak of diplomacy and take a few minutes to think about what will be the best and most calming way to deliver the bad news. Since no one in his right mind wants to hear bad news, expect the initial emotional reaction to be directed point blank at you. It won't matter that you are just the messenger. You will instantly become the symbol of whatever injustice the recipient thinks is being inflicted upon him, and because you are delivering the message, you obviously must be in cahoots with the sender. Don't look for logic. There is none when someone feels that he has been put on the defensive.

Whether it is a child, parent, administrator, teacher, coordinator, or a staff member who is the recipient of your message, it is important that you know your audience and frame what you have to say in a respectful and appropriate way. You would not talk to a child the way you would to a teacher or talk to an administrator like you would to a parent. Part of what you learn as a counselor is that at times like these, you may feel that you really are the orphan child of the building. There will be some teachers who wrongly think that you are a pseudo-administrator and resent having to listen to you, and there will be administrators who resent you if they feel that you are intervening into, or trying to influence, a situation with a child or parent who they are having an issue with. Remember Les Nessman's square on the floor? It is the proverbial line that they don't want you to cross.

It is particularly bothersome, too, when you have to deliver bad news to a parent in the place of a teacher or an administrator because instantly you have become the representative of the whole school who just "doesn't understand my child." Therefore, the recipient of Stage One of the parent's anger and resentment—guess who? Even if you bring with you helpful suggestions to alleviate the problem, you may be seen as an interloper for trying to intervene at all.

The feelings of resentment will usually pass as time goes by, and the situation will hopefully get resolved. However, I actually did have a parent who was so resentful when I was put in the position of trying to deal with her daughter's actions that she had me removed as her child's counselor. Talk about killing the messenger! This kind of situation is rare, but should it happen, don't take it personally. Sometimes people have to look for other people to blame when they think that they are being negatively judged, and you may become the unwanted beneficiary of their self-doubt.

There may be times when you feel that you are bombarded from several directions and that resentment is the "Word of the Day." No matter what you do, you just can't win. However, don't despair. Just because you may have to listen to the frustration of others doesn't mean that you have to *own* it. This is the key to dealing with anger and resentment. You can feel badly for them, but you are *not responsible* for these feelings in any way.

I know that it may be easier said than done, but often it is not what happens, but how you respond to it that can make or break your day. You will need to call upon your own objectivity when you are confronted with the reactions of other people. In many cases, you are just the messenger, so don't forget that. It is not in your job description to be verbally attacked by others for a decision that you may have had little or nothing to do with. People have a right to their feelings, but they don't have a right to bludgeon you with them. You may feel badly for them because sometimes it is warranted. However, you need to draw the line at a point when the conversation no longer contains any substantive matter and politely end the possible rant that the other person may be on. It's fine to let someone de-pressurize when they are upset, but there is a limit to that, too. To allow anger and shows of resentment to go on and on does not give that person an opportunity to become aware of his own behavior and get himself under control. It's like hitting a tennis ball up against a backboard nonstop. Some people can do it for hours.

Early in my career, I had a father raging in my office for a good fifteen minutes. I honestly couldn't get a word in edgewise. My director actually came and looked in my door to see if everything was okay. I chose to let him diffuse so that he hopefully wouldn't go home and take it out on his child, but looking back on it later that day, I realized that I had let his tirade go on way too long. He finally calmed down and apologized, but people out in the Counseling area could hear him, too. What I should have done when he began yelling was to stand up, walk to my door, and open it. This would have sent a signal that I was not going to allow the conference to continue. Then I should have told him that we would continue the conference with an administrator. This may or may not have settled him down, but it would have sent a clear message that tolerating his outrageous lack of self-control was not part of my job.

As counselors, we deal with many negative emotions. What I don't like about resentment is that sometimes it lingers long passed the issue that brought it into being. It can undermine relationships and be a destructive force to progress. It is best when recognized that you attempt to divert its influence through positive actions and make an effort to find a resolution to an issue, if it is at all possible.

Sometimes you will have no control over the situation or some people's attitude towards school counselors. If, however, you can find ways to constructively project your true role in the educational process, you will have a better chance of dispelling the misconceptions about who you are and why you are there. If anything, over time this can quell some of the resentment that others feel when you are forced to be the messenger.

Chapter 19: When Children Die

*"And as he was dreaming, an angel song
Awakened our Little Boy Blue—"*

Eugene Field
"Little Boy Blue", st. 2

Of all of the issues that a counselor must assist with, this for many is the hardest. There is something instinctive in us that believes that all children should have their chance to experience life, and if you are a parent, you know to the core of your being how devastating it would be to outlive your child. You would trade places with him or her in a heartbeat, if you could. This is when the emotional construct in all of us breaks down. No matter what your religious or spiritual beliefs are, we as human beings feel a shared sorrow when a child dies, and for a moment, if only fleeting, think that sometimes life can be so unfair.

From a child's point of view, the death of another child shakes the foundation of his world. "Kids don't die. If they can die, that means I could die." Suddenly, their own mortality becomes real. They can never return to the safe cocoon where death is what happens to other people, to old people, not to someone their age.

Depending on the circumstances of the child's death, there will be layers of other emotions beyond loss that will influence how you deal with this occurrence. For example, when a child has a terminal illness, there has been time for parents, teachers, and friends to try, if possible, to prepare for this eventual loss, even if they have emotionally denied what is happening. Dealing with this kind of death isn't any easier, but the shock of loss is not instantaneous. The shock and sadness are just as intense, but there is an inner knowing that this was a situation beyond anyone's control, and everything that could be done had been done. This death was inevitable but just as traumatic and heartbreaking.

When a child dies in an accident, the shock is acute. "This shouldn't have happened." "I don't understand." "This can't be real." "You've made a mistake." These are just some of the statements that you will hear. Their distress is extreme, especially for the close friends of the child. This kind of loss is very difficult to handle. You will be asked the question of *why did this happen* a hundred times, and you will have no way to give a satisfactory answer.

This is when *active listening* will be imperative so that you can formulate constructive answers according to what the child is feeling. You will need to think fast on your feet, and it can be very difficult. Use moments of silence to help them, as well as give yourself the time to decide what will be your best response. Sometimes the child will move on in the conversation even before you have had time to answer. <u>The truth is that we don't know why these things happen</u>. There is nothing wrong with saying this to a child. It is a realistic answer. The key is helping the child begin to assimilate this traumatic situation into his life and try to help him come to terms with the loss. Only time, family, friends, perhaps multiple visits to your office, and sometimes outside help will facilitate with this adjustment. This may only be the first step on a long path to healing and acceptance.

I had to deal several times in my career with multiple deaths at once (teenagers) due to a single car accident. When this happens, the Counseling Department won't be big enough to hold all of those who are grieving. In my experience, other schools were called upon to send some of their counselors on an emergency basis to help, and ministers who had received the news came to lend their services, as well. In a situation like this, there can't be too much help. Just make sure that administration has given approval to those who volunteer because they have assessed that these individuals are qualified to perform grief counseling.

As difficult and traumatic as the above situations are, the worst for me was when a child committed suicide. I did a lot of grief counseling over the years because when this happened, I was called to other schools, as well. This kind of senseless death seems to be beyond anyone's comprehension. To fear or avoid death is an imbedded concept in most people. It is why we instinctually protect ourselves from harm. How could a child be so desperate that he could face man's ultimate fear and cross that line? What unbelievable pain and anger must have been there for him to want to let go of everything at such a young age and in such a manner?

Oftentimes with young people, suicide is an impulsive act. What must they have experienced during their short life that could bring about such an inconceivable end? Although psychologists will tell you that this impulsivity happens more with boys, I have seen it among girls, as well. I can't describe it in any other way. It is heart-rending and mind-blowing. The suicide of a child, especially if you knew him or her, will change you forever. I will return to this subject later in this chapter.

So as a counselor, how do you go about handling the death of a child? Where do you even begin? The thought is overwhelming, particularly the first time that you have to deal with it. How you handle it can make a big difference in containing the hysteria of others, which can inundate you once the terrible news gets out. You must be prepared for the onslaught that is sure to come.

First and foremost, you will have to get your own emotions under control. This can be so very hard, particularly if the child was one of your own counselees, but you cannot help others manage their emotions if you can't manage your own. They are going to look to you to lean on during a time when they are questioning everything. If you are going to be able to perform your job, you will have to find your own individual way to put on a stoic face. Do whatever works for you. If the child was one of your close counselees, and your own distress is extreme, go into the faculty bathroom first and cry if you must to take the pressure off. Then compartmentalize your feelings and return to your office, focusing on the upset children and teachers who may already have begun to arrive.

I know that I am sounding simplistic, but what I am saying is realistic. This is part of your job, and no matter how difficult it is for you, you have to step up to the plate. Your feelings will have to be put on hold, or you will be no good to anyone. I am not trying to sound harsh. I am being practical. It is all right for the children to see that you are suffering, too, because you are a human being, but you must demonstrate it by your words and not tears if you are to be of any help to these children who are in shock and disbelief. It will probably be the most challenging situation in your job, but you must do it or leave the Counseling Department until you can. I say this without judgment and with understanding and compassion because I had to confront this situation myself. I hope that you will never have to deal with this crisis in your career, but you must be prepared for it, nonetheless.

So, how are we to control ourselves, you may wonder? Personally, the only way that I ever found to manage my own feelings was to create what I term as *tunnel vision*. I would make my outward focus so extreme that I could temporarily convince myself that the children or adults sitting in front of me were the only people in the whole universe and nothing else existed. In essence, I separated myself from myself as if my only purpose was to communicate with them. This may sound awfully strange to you, but it was the only way that I could compartmentalize my own feelings and keep my mind clear enough to talk to others and try to be of help. You will have to find your own way to handle your emotions. Creative visualization was how I handled mine. Each time I dealt with a child's death, I strengthened this survival skill. I never got used to the death of a child, but I got used to handling myself. That's all we can really do as counselors.

It is unfortunate that during the time when you will be needed most, you yourself may be very vulnerable, too, but you must find your own way to cope. You must focus outward and solely on the children or adults who are grieving.

Hopefully, your school has a plan in place for how to deal with large numbers of children in distress. We had a conference room that was used if there were too many grieving children in the Counseling Office.

I think that it is important to discuss here the kinds of scenarios that can appear around you due to the death of a child. I have divided them into levels, not to sound cold or surgical, but for clarification.

Level I- Close Friends of the Child

These children are usually so distressed that they will ask to call a parent to immediately come pick them up from school. If they don't, you still need to make parental contact and put the child on the phone with the one you can reach. The parent is their root. It always seems to calm them down.

I still suggest that they be sent home with their parent if at all possible. There is no way that these children will be able to function for the rest of the school day, and the clinic can't take them. Most parents will be willing to pick their child up or give permission through an administrator to have their child go home with the parent of another friend. Just follow protocol for the release of a child to someone who is not her parent. Always involve administration.

Level II- Classmates and Acquaintances

These kids have the difficult task of looking over at an empty chair where their classmate used to sit. Even if they didn't particularly like the child, it is a terrible feeling to know that the chair will remain empty. Some teachers actually remove the chair from the classroom. My feelings are torn about this. I can see the positives and negatives of doing this, but either way, there will still be an empty space.

In some cases, you may be asked to follow the schedule of the deceased child and tell each class what has happened. Also, you will be doing a form of generalized grief counseling. In many cases, the class will be stunned to silence, with only one or two children able to voice a question or concern. That's okay. You explained the true story and tried to quell any rumors that will surely get passed around. Also, too, just making yourself available will open the door to students who may not have been willing to talk during class about what has happened. They may come in privately to see you or their own counselor later.

I once had a child laugh when I informed a class of the death of one of their classmates. Although it was inappropriate, some children will respond in a socially unacceptable way because they are afraid of their own feelings, especially because the child who died is the same age as they are, and this may be a new experience for them altogether. They just don't know how to react, so laughing can be their way of being in denial. Keep this in mind, and try not to acknowledge any inappropriate responses with negative words. The other students will already be horrified enough by such a reaction.

You may also find some students will come to see you because they feel guilty about not liking the student who died or may have had past confrontations with him. These children carry an added burden on their shoulders.

Most of the deceased child's classmates will tend to stay in school once they get over the initial shock. However, judge whether any individuals need to talk to a parent, and always ask them if they think that they can stay in school or do they feel that they need to go home.

Level III- Students Who Didn't Know the Child Who Died but are Reacting to the Others Who are Grieving

Some children are emotionally sensitive to the environment around them. If others are upset, they think that they should be upset, too. Some will just be reacting to the death of someone their own age. Others may be reconnecting with another personal loss. These are the children who you should be able to get back to class after you reassure them that everything is under control, and yes, it is very sad but everyone is being taken care of and will be all right. If, however, you know that a particular student is emotionally unstable or is receiving outside counseling for depression or loss, put the child on the phone with a parent and let the parent make a judgment call on whether or not the child should remain in school.

Level IV- Kids Who Use this Situation to Get Out of Class

Yes, it's sad but true. I saw this more often with teenagers, though. There are some kids who will use any situation to get out of class. However, they will be relatively easy to spot. Grief or shock will not be on their faces, or they may try to mimic it by overreacting. Either way, within a few minutes you will be able to pick them out of the crowd. They will be socializing with other people and try to stretch out their stay in Counseling as long as they can. The way we usually handled this was to give the child some time, perhaps a half hour, and then ask these children if they wanted to call a parent to come get them or return to class. Make these their *only* two options. "I want to stay here" is not an option.

When you say "No," expect a resentful or angry response because they would love to hang out with their friends until lunchtime. I actually had a whole group of kids try to do this once. Their angry responses but unwillingness to call a parent was a sure indicator that they were trying to pull a fast one. You just don't have time to keep all of these children when so many others are genuinely grieving. Rarely did one of these kids ever call a parent, and when she did, it was very uncommon for a parent to leave work to come pick the child up. The parent would tell the child to go back to class.

I had no problem letting the parent appear to be the bad guy in these situations. We would write passes for these children and send them on their way. Boy, were they ticked off and oftentimes quiet verbal in their discontent. This was always another telling sign of their insincerity.

Teachers Who are Grieving

The longest day in a teacher's life is to have to continue to teach after she has learned of the death of one of her students. I have witnessed amazing strength in so many teachers in the face of such a tragedy, but it is a particularly hard loss for them because they had a daily relationship with the child, and they must, as you must, try to control their emotions to help their grieving students.

During the class that has lost the student, the teacher will be the one to deal with the empty chair. Obviously, there will probably be no teaching, just talking or trying to hold things together, sometimes with the help of a counselor if one can be freed up to follow the child's class schedule. The rest of the day will probably be an attempt on the teacher's part to answer the other students' questions and then try to redirect the class to some form of a quiet activity in an effort to control and stabilize the day. Having experienced this as a teacher myself, I can tell you that this can be an overwhelming and emotionally exhausting task.

Amidst all the counseling that you are doing for the grieving children, try to find times during the day to check on the child's teachers. Some may have to leave the classroom for a few minutes off and on to be able to keep their emotions under control. Hopefully, colleagues who have a planning period at that time will step in for these teachers while they take a breather as they must continue to keep themselves under control. If you are free, offer to step in if needed and take over a class for awhile yourself.

Some teachers will come to your office during their planning period or after school. Helping them is just as important as helping the children. Loss is loss, no matter what the relationship. Most teachers will be able to handle the situation, but some are fragile human beings who may have suffered such a loss in their family, and these individuals can be overwhelmed. The bottom line is to do whatever you have to do to help everyone get through the day.

****

Please Note:

I would like to briefly state that if you ever have to deal with the situation of a child who has been murdered (Thankfully, I only had two instances of this, and the children were former students and no longer in our school), I suggest that you do some reading on this type of grief counseling. It is in a category all its own due to the violence connected to the act. I hope that you all will never have to deal with this.

****

Suicides

The only other topic that I would like to cover in this chapter is to return to the subject of suicide. I have known counselors to leave the profession because they could not handle this kind of death. It really is the worst thing to have to deal with, especially if the child was one of your own counselees. There are no easy answers, and there are so many questions left unanswered. If you can handle this, you can handle anything.

If there is anything that I can say that may be of help and that you can pass on to others, it is this: the problems that eventually drove this child to commit such a desperate act existed long before you or anyone else at school entered the picture. I remember clearly sitting in a conference room full of teachers who were distraught over the death of one of their students. They had all taken the child "under their wing," for some months and had been in regular contact with the parents, who unfortunately were in denial. Everyone was now second-guessing themselves, including the child's counselor. "Could I have done more?" "Would she have killed herself if I hadn't been absent yesterday?" "Why didn't the parents believe that their child was capable of this?" On and on the questions went, and yet the answer was still the same. When the child made her final decision, there was no more warning and no sharing of this infor-mation. It was a plan that was constructed silently over time and sadly, carried out when it was least expected. The signs had been seen and dealt with but to no avail.

Suicide is a tragedy beyond words, but we have to find a way to accept it. No one can know the inner workings of another one's mind. If we could, there would be no suicides. All any of us can do is be watchful and immediately deal with self-destructive behavior, such as *cutting* or other manifestations, and report the behaviors to the parents and school nurse immediately. Involve the school psychologist, if possible. Pull out all of the stops on this one. If you don't, you may be questioning yourself for the rest of your life, even though the problems of the child existed long before you.

Please don't torment yourself. It is emotionally scarring and self-destructive. Always remember, you will never be able to take on the pain of others, and you will only be able to help the ones who will let you. Sadly, some children will never open that door for you or anyone else's help.

In dealing with the questions most asked, here are some of the answers I gave. They may or may not work for you. When asked why the person did this (only one student in all of my years of grief counseling left an explicit note), I was very frank with the students and told them that only that person knew the true answer to this question, and it is something that we may never know. For whatever reason, he must have lost hope. I also added, though (and I said this to more than one grieving parent, as well), that I truly believed that if the child could have seen past his pain and could have taken a moment to truly think about his choice and of the repercussions to the others that he would be leaving behind, he would have made a different decision. Sometimes saying this remark was the only solace that I could give to anyone. I also believe that this is a true statement, since so many suicides among children are impulsive acts.

My Personal Choice Regarding Viewings and Funerals

When attending the viewing or the funeral of a child who had committed suicide (In general, I usually chose the evening viewing so that I could be in school to work with the children on the day of the funeral (my personal choice), I would say to the parent the only words that I knew how to say, and they were from the heart: "I wish that I had the right words to say to you, but I don't." In the case of a suicide, I also repeated the same statement from the above paragraph about believing that the child would have made a different decision if he had understood the pain and repercussions of his act.

Even if you are feeling anger towards the parents because you had tried to warn them, and they didn't take proper action or refused to accept the possibility of this happening, you will need to reach deep down inside of yourself and draw upon your own humanity. These parents have lost their child and most will be blaming themselves for the rest of their life. Nothing will ever be the same. Even if the parents tried to do everything they could, they will still feel that they have failed, and even if you may inwardly feel (out of anger at the parents' blindness) that they deserve to feel guilty, this negative attitude will turn on you and become a self-punishment to which there is no exit. No matter what the circumstances are that may have lead to this wretched situation, let compassion and not judgment be your guide because everyone will have to come to terms and find their own way to heal.

There is no easy way to end this chapter. Over the years I have tried to console myself and others with one enduring thought. Although someone's journey on this earth may have been shorter than the expected years, no one passes through without affecting our lives in some way. Their legacy may not be in years, but it will be in how they touched our lives and how we may have touched theirs. Sometimes someone who lived a short life can touch us just as deeply as one who lived a long one, and maybe more. Recognize this, and be thankful for the time you were given to know them. **Please always share this thought with the parents.**

Chapter 20: Sometimes You Win, Sometimes You Lose…(but you've got to dress out for the game)

"You win a few, you lose a few. Some get rained out. But you got to dress for all of them."

Satchel Paige
Baseball player

I suppose everyone either consciously or unconsciously keeps some kind of track record in their head as they travel up the hills and down into the valleys of their career. Each of us has his own way of equating what we would label as successes or failures in our attempts to bring significance to our job. Counselors are no different. We all seek to be successful in our chosen profession.

One major difference, however, between our job and that of other professions is that we cannot always see the results of our work because we are dealing with the various aspects of the human psyche, which cannot be measured in concrete terms. Whether we have been successful or not with helping another human being can only be assumed by observing whether or not a person's future actions and decisions-making demonstrates a positive and, hopefully, lasting behavioral change. Sometimes we don't even have the opportunity to observe this because the changes being made may be reflected more at home than at school.

Having been a teacher for fifteen years, I could much too easily slip into grading myself by the outcome of this situation or that one. If I had a string of less than encouraging outcomes, accompanied usually by being both mentally and physically tired, there would exist in my head a modified grading scale: everything became either an "A" if it was successful or an "F" if it was not. Forget about any grade for a partial success. It was at these times that I would have to step back and realize that I had totally lost my perspective in my job.

First of all, if you catch yourself grading yourself, acknowledge that your personal objectivity has temporarily flown out of the window when you need it most. Take time to recognize that the ground under your feet will always be changing. Sometimes you will get positive feedback from a parent or child. Then again, you may get shut out of the process completely and never know for sure if you helped them at all. Sometimes you will receive negative feedback, particularly from those children or adults who have refused to take personal responsibility for their own actions. Both counselors and teachers are easy targets to become "the fall guy" because we dared to care enough to intervene while those involved weren't motivated enough to change.

There were times during my career when I would question whether or not I was making any kind of difference at all in the lives of the children with whom I worked. These were the times when I had to catch myself being much too judgmental of myself in my own head and of my ability to do my job competently. Try to keep in mind that there will be successes, as well as what you might personally label as failures (change your judgmental label of *failure* to *a less than hoped for outcome*), and these disappointments will sometimes happen in back-to-back succession. It can be discouraging, but you haven't lost your game. It's really just the "luck of the draw." It would be wonderful if positive and not so positive outcomes could alternate so we would not feel out of balance in our job sometimes, but that's not the way it goes. It is what it is, and you do have to dress out for the next game, even when you may have temporarily given in to self-doubt.

Get your perspective back by remembering that human beings tend to maintain the *status quo* because it takes effort and often hard work to change, and change can be painful. Most situations that you will be dealing with will only show improvement over time. Often with children, you will see them take two steps forward and one step back. It is so hard to change behavior at any age.

If you feel that you must take measure, the fact that a person is *trying to change* is how you should quantify whether or not you have successfully helped someone. To make an immediate assessment after dealing with a child's or adult's issue will usually lead to disappointment because we know that people don't magically change overnight.

Remember that there is a big difference between judging yourself and evaluating your progress in your job. It is important to evaluate what strategies work and don't work, refine your skills as you gain from your daily experiences, and remain flexible in your approaches so that you can grow as the job grows. There is no grade for success or failure with this. As with everyone, each of us is a work in progress and we, as counselors, should afford ourselves the same patience and understanding that we give so freely to others.

One strategy that I was taught to use by one of my directors (Susan) when I had those times of feeling unsuccessful was to keep a folder with all of the notes, letters, drawings, cards, and other offerings that I had received over the months and years from a thankful child, parent, teacher, or anyone who claimed that I had helped them in their time of need. Looking through that folder when you feel dejected really will help you regain your perspective on why you are there, and why you stay, even when you will sometimes question your own abilities.

It really is not about winning or losing but that you show up and give it your best. In the big picture of things, your part is to give someone a tool that he can use to initiate a change in his life, but in the end, it is up to the individual whether or not he chooses to use it.

Chapter 21: Give Options, Not Advice

"Advice is seldom welcome, and those who want it most always like it least."

Philip Dormer Stanhope,
Earl of Chesterfield
Letters, January 29, 1748

It is so hard not to give advice. It seems to be the natural thing to do because most of us have opinions and often like to share them with others. However, by giving our opinion, we are either directly or indirectly giving other people our advice. Advice doesn't always have to be preceded by the words, "I think that you should…" Having a strong opinion can indirectly influence someone's decision, and if we are being honest with ourselves, we have all been guilty of directly influencing someone by our indirect but powerful words and gestures. Body language sells, and we use it to emphasize a point. We know what we are doing, and we often do it on purpose.

I, for one, had to watch myself all of the time. Having also been a classroom teacher for so many years before I became a counselor, I had to be doubly careful not to be strongly directive in my working with counselees. Telling students what they needed to do had become ingrained as part of my communication skills, and I had to fight this urge through constant self-awareness throughout my counseling career. I basically had to unlearn my *modus operandi.*

It is important to remember that with advice comes responsibility. By giving advice, you bind yourself to the outcome if the person who you are advising decides to use it. If things go well, that's great. You may receive praise, or the person may take all of the credit for himself. It doesn't really matter. Let him take the credit. However, if things don't go as hoped, well, … Although the negative outcome may be for reasons other than your advice, you can bet that you will become part of the collateral damage when it goes wrong. "I took your advice and look what happened!" That's not something you want to land in your office. You have enough to deal with already.

Again, giving advice falls under the category of the *quick fix*, and we have talked about that already. It is tempting to do this when you have so many others who are waiting to see you or six parent phone calls to return, but it can backfire on you. It is particularly unpleasant if the child goes home and tells a parent that you said to do something and the parent disagrees. It is also unpleasant if the child goes home and tells a parent a confused version of what you said. Even if it wasn't advice, a child can make it sound that way. To receive an angry early morning phone call that starts off, "Did you tell my child to…? !"

is not the way you want to start your day. To have to answer with, "No, Sir. That is *not* what I told your child to do." puts you in a weakened position because you are being forced to explain yourself, and the parent will likely believe his child before he believes you.

You mustn't be anxious about every word you say. Just keep in mind that it will be to your own benefit and for all of those you counsel, including parents, if you train yourself to answer the question, "What do you think I should do?" with these two responses in this order: (Reflect back) "What do *you* think that *you* might do to help solve this problem?" (very empowering), and then, "How do *you* think that I *might* help you?" Then you can add, "Here are *several additional options that you might want to think about*." Make these two questions part of your automatic response routine, and you will find that you may avoid a lot of potential pitfalls that can appear unexpectedly in your path.

These responses will also work equally well when you are doing group counseling. Asking the individual child to initiate a solution to his problem will redirect the focus from the group and back onto that individual, requesting that he think about options that may work for him. This will keep the child from automatically accepting the options that the other group members may be suggesting or considering for themselves.

Using this technique kept me from falling back into the learned habit of giving a *directed response* from my former teaching days. Hopefully, this method will help you, too.

Chapter 22: The Grab Bag- Practical Strategies

"Our life is frittered away by detail...Simplify, simplify."

Henry David Thoreau

I have been looking forward to writing this chapter because it is not going to be like any of the others. To write this chapter forced me to spend a day going back through the numerous personal counselor logs that I had kept over the years in case I ever decided to write a book. I do want to stress that these logs listed *names* and the words *personal* or *academic* after each child's name and usually a short description, such as *grade concern* or had *argument with friend* and **did not** include confidential counselor notes. Those notes and files were destroyed before I retired. No children's names have been used in this book.

Perusing the logs gave me a global view of my career. It was interesting when I discovered how a name could bring back a young face or situation that I hadn't thought about in years. Some of these people and situations had both taught me and touched my life. Whether I had learned something about that person, about one's relationship to oneself and others, about the two sides of human nature, or about myself, knowing these people had helped me to grow as a human being, and I can only hope that I did the same for them. When I am done with this book, I will destroy these logs, as well. This is the ethical thing to do.

Note: *Some professionals believe that counselor logs should be destroyed at the end of each school year or they become data. Check for any requirements of your individual school district. In my case, I kept some of my logs that listed names and not personal details to be referred to as examples for this book.*

I have spent a lot of this book so far talking about issues that you will confront in your job, many of which center on you as a counselor first before you can even begin to deal with the issues of others. This is important because you will be a work in progress everyday of your career. People will come in and out of your life, and their lives and stories will change you and help you to grow both as a counselor and as a person. However, that being said, it's time to get practical.

I call this chapter "The Grab Bag" for a reason. In reading through my old logs, I realized that although circumstances varied, many situations were just variations on a theme. Because of this, I decided to group them within categories. They run the gamut from dealing with kids, parents, teachers, administrators, academics, social problems, relationship issues---just about anything you can think of—at least, anything that I could think of. I may explain a strategy I used, something that I observed about a counselee or her parents, something that I did in an effort to resolve a problem (which may or may not have worked well), and things that you might want to think about.

I chose five major categories and discuss six out of the many possible topics under each one (I could go on and on and never cover them all). These topics aren't placed in any particular order, except that I have attempted to loosely group them under the appropriate category. However, as you will see, some will crisscross several areas at once, so I chose what I thought was the more logical placement. They will just be a grab bag of observations and ideas. I hope that some of them will help you or spur you on to develop your own strategies because you may not necessarily agree with my point of view, or perhaps how I handled a particular situation may not work for you. By developing your own bag of tools that you have discovered are successful for you, you are less likely to get hung up by the details that can waste valuable time and sometimes impede any progress.

Parent Issues

*Multi-cultural Issues- It is important to know the ethnic make-up of your school from the very beginning. Even if you are working in a school that has only a few different cultures, you may find that not knowing the cultural expectations of a child's parent can sometimes hinder finding a solution to the problem. Find out whether or not it is the father or the mother whose role it is to tend to their child's education. This is very important because that will most likely be the person who shows up in your office when there is a concern. Realize that the progress may sometimes be slower if the mother is not allowed to make a decision without the approval of the father, who is the head of the family.

Although we can only speculate and perhaps generalize, the religious beliefs of a given culture are imbedded in a child's cultural upbringing and belief system, as it is in any country, and the parents' response to an issue may be quite different than in this country. Be knowledgeable, sensitive, and aware of whom you are dealing with and gain information by listening to their choice of words and watching body language as they talk to you or interact with their child. This will provide you with even more detailed information about how to appropriately work with whatever issue that the parent has brought to your office.

*<u>Health Issues</u>- It is obvious that having a child with a chronic health issue is a constant stress on a parent. Although it is rarely if ever stated out loud, a mother, in particular, can feel guilty or responsible for what has happened to her son or daughter, even though she had nothing to do with the condition or illness. This can cause a heighten sensitivity on the parent's part when anything occurs that is negatively affecting her child.

I had the pleasure of working with some of the most remarkable and inspiring parents who helped their children positively cope with their health issues by empowering them to deal with it as a challenge and not an obstacle. These children and parents were amazing role models for us all.

On the other end of the spectrum, there were parents who viewed both themselves and their child as victims and basically tried to intimidate, bully, and threaten anyone who had any contact with their child if things didn't go their way ALL OF THE TIME. In many cases, it was the mother of the child, and the term ferocious "Mama Bear" was more than an appropriate description. With some, there was no reasoning with them. They were determined to get their way and warned, "I will take it to the Superintendent and the School Board if I have to!" After enough threat-filled meetings, you may find your compassionate side beginning to ebb a little. Just remain professional when this happens.

At this point, if you haven't already, don't have a meeting with the parent without an administrator. The minute a parent tries to intimidate or bully you, tell them that this is a decision that needs an administrator because you do not have the authority to make it. Don't look at this as a coward's way out or passing the buck. That's what the "pecking order" is there for. Let the administrator intervene. This type of parent is used to bullying teachers and school counselors, but they usually calm down when an administrator is present (but not always). Having someone connected to administration helps to alleviate the pressure on you and the teacher because the truth is, an administrator may have to be the one who makes a decision about what the parents want done. You and the teacher may sometimes be disappointed with the outcome, but parents like this will go above your head all of the time. Don't be insulted, but also don't be bullied.

Even if the parent does eventually go to the Superintendent, you can bet it won't be for the first or last time. Some will have made themselves known to the Superintendent long before you. The problem will just get kicked back to your school principal or to a supervisor for special needs students, who will then get an administrator, any teachers involved, and the counselor to set up another meeting. Don't let a parent like this scare you. Stay centered, even though you are so aggravated, and remember that you are there as an advocate for the child. What's best for the student is what matters, not who wins or loses the battle.

*Parent Conferences- Conferences with parents and teachers can be one of the strongest and most beneficial tools that you have to bring about an under-standing between the parent, the teachers, and the child (sometimes the parent or teachers will request that the child attend). Communication is essential for solving any kind of issue.

Unless an administrator has been requested to be in attendance, you, the counselor, will be the one to head the meeting, except in the case of the teacher requesting the meeting and inviting you. It will also be your respon-sibility to control it. If you anticipate that a parent/teacher conference may be difficult due to past parent contact or teacher feedback, you may want to meet with the teachers prior to the conference so that everyone can stay focused and have both the small and big picture of the child's academic and behavioral performance.

From the parent's point of view, one of the things that can really aggravate him is when he has requested a meeting and some of the teachers don't show up. I don't blame the parent for being upset. It is very unprofessional and not acceptable, unless the teacher is absent from school.

Make sure that you send an email or place a notice in each teacher's box when a Parent/Teacher Conference is requested, scheduling the conference for at least several days later so that it will not conflict with any previously scheduled meeting or conference that they might have. Ask for a verification of the date from each teacher. Send a final reminder the day before the conference.

If you find that several of the teachers have conflicts with the conference date, speak to the parent about rescheduling the conference so that all of the teachers will be able to attend. If one teacher cannot attend but all others can, ask the teacher to send grades, comments, observations, and an explanation of what the child needs to do to be successful in the class (such as do his/her homework, study for tests, stop socializing with classmates, etc.) so that a plan of action can be discussed during the parent conference. If the child is failing in this teacher's class, ask the parent if you can set up a separate parent/teacher conference on another day, or if he would like the teacher who is absent to phone him.

You need to keep your own documentation during the meeting, asking questions and making possible suggestions based on the information that is given by each teacher and the parent responses. You will then be able to refer to those notes if the parent calls back and claims that the teacher never told him certain information because he may be looking for a way out for his child not finishing an assignment (It happens!). This protects you, the teacher, and provides documentation about the meeting for an administrator who may get called in to settle any dispute between the parent and teacher. **Document, document, document.**

If a meeting becomes volatile and accusatory on the parent's part, calmly intervene immediately. Remind the parent that you realize that emotions are high because he is so worried about his child but that we are all meeting because we want his child to be successful, too, so we need to keep focused on helpful strategies. If the parent continues to be in any way abusive towards you or any teacher, announce that you see no positive outcome to this meeting, and you will be rescheduling it for another time when an administrator can be present. Then thank the teachers for attending and excuse them. Never let an upset or abusive parent control a conference. It is part of _your_ job to control the atmosphere in the meeting.

Next, go immediately to the appropriate administrator and tell her that you shut down a parent conference due to a verbally abusive parent because no progress was being made. Don't let the parent be the one who let's the administrator know what has happened. No one appreciates being blind-sided by an angry parent phone call. It makes you look bad and the administrator, too, and gives the parent a chance to say to the administrator, "Obviously, the school doesn't care about my child because you don't even know about what happened!" Administrators really appreciate it if you give them warning that they may be receiving an angry phone call or some form of a complaint because a parent conference had to be terminated. Then request that the administrator attend the next parent meeting with you and the teachers and turn over the reins to her so she will become the new sounding board. This is part of her job description, and she is the next step in dealing with an unruly parent.

Remember that neither you nor any teacher is paid to be verbally bludgeoned by an emotionally out-of-control parent who is looking to blame others because he is frustrated or not taking parental responsibility. Just don't take it personally. Observe the parent so that you can gain a better view of why the child is the way he is. It will be very beneficial to have this information when working with this student in the future. In the process, you may also discover if a parent is being abusive towards his child, but NEVER jump to conclusions and be VERY careful. Just because a parent has a bad temper DOES NOT mean that he is physically harming his child.

*Referring an Issue to an Administrator- Knowing when to bring an administrator in to solve a problem with a student or parent may vary according to your school system and/or an individual school's regulations or expectations. It is very important to know where the counselor stands in the chain-of-command in dealing with any number of issues that may, on any given day, land at your door.

Just as many teachers prefer to handle their own classroom discipline problems when possible (I did) and only involve an administrator when all else fails, you may feel this way as a school counselor, too. To strive for acquiring the skills to handle all of the issues that are brought to you is a noble endeavor, but remember that we all have limitations, whether they are self-imposed or subject to the authority of others. Understand very clearly where administration draws the line on what belongs in a counselor's domain and what is an administrative issue. You aren't meant to do it all. You do not want to cross over into areas that are not delegated to you. There is a good reason for this. Stepping outside of your designated boundary can open you up to, at the very least, administrative censure or, at worse, a lawsuit against you or the school system.

I am not stating this as a scare tactic. I am just trying to keep you from being a Don Quixote, no matter how well-intentioned you are. This type of situation isn't likely to happen often, but it can be a miserable experience if it does happen. Never be afraid to ask for advice if you are unsure where you stand in a questionable situation. Consult with your counseling director and administration and document the date and what was said. Follow whatever instructions are given to you by those who are in authority, even if it means that you hand over the issue for administration to handle. Don't take offense or let your ego tell you that the administrator should trust you to handle the problem. It has nothing to do with ego or self-esteem. It has to do with trying to find a positive resolution to the problem, and the person who solves it may not be you.

*Keeping your Expectations of Parents in Check- If you are wondering why I use the words, "in check," I have no doubt that it won't take long for you to experience the utter frustration that every counselor feels after you have invested so much time working with not only a child, but generating strategies for a parent to implement and see absolutely NO improvement in the situation. There is nothing more aggravating than to spend hours and hours with a parent on the phone and in parent/teacher or counselor conferences, both scheduled and unscheduled (they tend to show up unannounced) and find yourself repeating over and over again *ad infinitum* the same suggestions and available options. All of the parent's ongoing tears and/or angst can wear thin on a counselor's compassion when you feel that all the time and effort you have given to help this parent and her child may as well have been tossed to the wind.

When you see the parent coming down the hall yet again, possibly unannounced, and in your head, you hear a tiny little voice say, "Oh, no! Not again—not today," remember that you are human, too, and have your own tolerance level. Then put on your welcoming smile and draw upon your active listening skills and ask specific but open-ended questions and try to glean from the parent if she has tried to initiate **any** of the strategies that you have already presented to her. Then you will save yourself what will amount to wasted time repeating all of the same options yet again.

It is so simple for us to be judgmental in this kind of situation because we just can't figure out why some parents don't or won't follow through. You may wonder, "If she wasn't going to use any of the strategies, why did she come to see me in the first place, and why does she keep coming back?" Well, there are many reasons. Most parents are very sincere in wanting to make things better for their child, but they may not have the skills to do it. Some parents have self-esteem issues, some have a spouse who undermines all of their efforts, some won't buy into *tough love* because they think that they will lose the love of their child, some have been manipulated by family members their whole life (including their children), some don't want to put forth the effort to correct the situation because it will be too difficult and they just want to complain, some just need attention, and some just want you to do all the hard parenting for them. The list of reasons goes on and on.

All you can really do is try to get the parent (or parents) on the same page if you can. Try to create a plan one strategy at a time that you and the parent agree to follow. Attempt to initiate a conference with the parent's spouse, too, and see if you can generate some kind of agreed-upon parental consistency. As the old saying goes, "You can take a horse to water, but you can't make him drink it." Keep your parental expectations in check and realistic so that you hold down your own level of frustration and maybe disappointment, and keep chipping away at whatever issue a parent may continually bring to your door.

Building long term and positive relationships with the parents of students who have ongoing issues is your best chance for promoting constructive change for the student. Sometimes just letting the parents and child know that you care and that your door is always open (even if you find they use your office just to vent) is the best that you can do short term in the hope of eventually bringing about some long term change.

*<u>Reporting Parents (or Others) to Social Services</u>- I always found that having to make a call to Social Services regarding the possible safety of a child was the easiest and hardest thing that I had to do in my job description. It was easy in that it was my legal and moral duty to report any *suspected abuse* and hard because I knew that there could be severe ramifications within the family structure, even if the claim was deemed *unfounded.* However, this is not the counselor's judgment call or concern. Make the call when there is suspected abuse. A counselor cannot be sued for making a report, even if it is proven to be unfounded, but you can be sued if you suspected abuse and did not report it.

It was not unusual for children who appeared in my office with bruises and other marks from physical abuse to beg me not to make a report because they were afraid of the repercussions at home when their parents found out. It took time to convince them that under the law I had no choice but to make sure that they were protected, and that once Social Services intervened, parents knew that the law was watching and the battle lines had been drawn. Some children understood and were thankful to talk to somebody about what was going on, particularly when they were worried about their younger siblings. Unfortunately with others, my relationship with them was permanently damaged. Sadly, this last scenario can sometimes happen, but you don't have a choice.

The main thing to keep in mind is making a report to Social Services becomes your responsibility when it is brought into your office, unless the regulations of your school system delegate this responsibility to a principal or school nurse. It is on your shoulders until you make that phone call. It then becomes the responsibility of the social worker to decide how the situation is going to be handled.

In my experience physical abuse that had left marks on the child warranted a visit that day from one of our social workers. Emotional abuse, however, was the most frustrating situation. It can be as destructive long term as some physical abuse, but unfortunately, marks on the child's psyche can't be photographed and, therefore, are very hard to prove. Our social workers would still take the report, though, and keep it on file so that a record could be established if the emotional abuse escalated to physical abuse or was ongoing to the point that numerous reports had been filed.

As far as parental reactions towards you as the child's counselor, I found that in a majority of cases, the parents never made any contact with me, even if the child told them that I was the one who called. I would imagine that it was because they had either been found out or they were mortified. That was not my problem. I was the advocate for the child. It was up to the parents to prove their guilt or innocence to Social Services, not to me.

If they did contact me or show up at my office upset, I explained that I made no judgment in reference to whether or not the information was truthful but that I was required by law to make a report and, therefore, had no option in the matter. I informed them that it was now out of my hands and then referred them back to Social Services.

I did hear of instances where a parent threatened a school counselor (it was not in our school system), but it was relatively rare and extreme. Of course, should you ever have this happen, don't hesitate to tell your principal and immediately file a police report. Having an officer show up at their home will no doubt cool the parent's temper pretty quickly. I really believe that the chance of this happening during your career is slim and none, but NEVER hesitate to document and bring in the authorities for your own protection. However, <u>don't try to investigate the claim yourself</u>. And remember, always err on the side of the child and his safety. It is up to Social Services and the law to figure out the rest.

Academic Issues

Special Children- Perhaps each of these categories of children should be talked about separately, but I grouped them here because you will find that whatever school system you work for will have different procedures, guidelines, and educational programs designed for special children, whether they are gifted or have a disability.

*Special Education- Of course, children who have an IEP (Individualized Education Plan) are protected under federal guidelines, even though how the IEP is implemented will, to a certain extent, depend on what resources the school system is able to offer. That, of course, depends on money. Usually the higher the tax base in a community, the more the city or county system can offer the child through specialized programs and other resources. One way or another, federal guidelines must be met.

Make sure that you learn the process for making a referral for a child to be evaluated for possible special education. Parents will ask you, and teachers and administrators will come with concerns that a child might need testing.

Unless it is against procedure in your school system, try to go to as many of your counselees IEP meetings as possible. It is important to learn of the child's needs and if there are any other problems. Your input is important, and some-times the counselor will be asked to be part of the solution. It will also give you a current overall view of the child's progress because there will be current teacher reports, which will give you the information needed to meet with the child yourself and track his progress.

*ESL (English as a Second Language)- ESL has federal guidelines, as well. Depending on the school system in which you work (money being the decider again), you may have only one ESL teacher who is shared between your school and one other, or you may have more than one full-time teacher assigned to your school. In any case, it is important to keep in contact with the ESL teacher and voice any concerns that arise.

The regular classroom teacher can become extremely frustrated when teaching an ESL child because she sincerely wants to help the child, but she is also responsible for teaching all of the other children in class. The teacher can feel torn and sometimes a little overwhelmed when she has to split her responsibilities between her English and non-English speaking students. ESL teachers coordinate with the regular classroom teachers and will make you aware of the child's needs by keeping you in the loop of communication.

I occasionally had an ESL child become very depressed because he felt like "a stranger in a strange land." I didn't blame him. To be plopped into the middle of a different culture and not be able to speak the language must be pretty scary. Get to know these children and send notes to their teachers to try to buddy the child with someone in each of his classes and at lunch so the child won't feel so isolated. This can work wonders with an ESL student's adjustment to his new environment. It is particularly helpful if you can buddy him with another student from the same culture who has already learned a lot of English or was raised bilingual, especially if both of them can have the same lunch.

We all know that being alone in the lunchroom can be very intimidating. When possible, I would initially set a child's schedule (at least one or two classes and lunch) to match another ESL student's so the child would hopefully have an instant buddy built into his day. Teachers really appreciate this, too, because the other student can translate concepts to the new child in his own language. Be creative and find whatever ways you can to connect the ESL child to his new school.

*Gifted Children- The gifted can have their own set of issues. It's great if you have a Gifted Program in your school. Of course, there are procedures, specific criteria, and usually batteries of tests that children must take in order to be classified as "gifted" in an area of study.

There are special programs in which the child may be pulled from her regular class as often as once a week or sometimes programs where she may participate in all gifted or advanced classes. Again, how much money the school system can allot for special programs is usually the determining factor.

If I saw any common issue among many of these children, it was that they could often be such perfectionists that they would fall apart if they didn't get straight "A's". Keep this in mind, and if you see this in a student, have a conference with the child and the parent(s). Determine if the child is pressuring himself due to his personality construct, living in the shadow of a perfect sibling, or suffocating under the demands of parent expectations. This will help you decide how you might diffuse some of the stress by trying to have a meeting of the minds.

And, of course, never forget all of the truly gifted children who are, and will never be, part of a gifted program. One of my most gifted counselees was a special education (LD) child who has since gone on to become a wonderful graphic artist. Being gifted has little to do with grades because some of the most gifted children will never display their special talent while sitting in the straight rows of a traditional classroom setting. When you discover these children, find opportunities for them to shine and encourage them to expand their special gift(s) by showing their work to others, unless a child refuses. Don't let his light stay hidden under a barrel. Show this child that you believe in him.

As I said in a previous chapter, I did not have a formal, hang-your-diploma-on-the-wall kind of office. I had all kinds of posters, knick-knacks, stuffed animals, and student artwork and poems covering almost every surface. Even the high school students loved my office, and I don't apologize for my choice. Watch a kid's face light up when you recognize his special gift.

You may be the only one in the school who knows his talent exists because he chose you to be the one to see it. I always told these children that it was an honor to display their work in my office because sometimes they have had little or no positive reinforcement at home or by their peers, so it is really an act of trust for them to share it with you.

*Attendance Issues- How involved you are with tracking your counselees' attendance will depend on the requirements of your job description in your particular school system. Usually there is an Office of Attendance which tracks the overall attendance for the school system and breaks it down school by school, but it is usually up to the individual school to deal with their own chronic attendance problems.

Whoever handles the daily attendance in your school (often an Attendance Secretary) will let you know if a child has reached the designated number of missed days that the school system (usually based on your state's regulations) considers unacceptable. In some cases, your school may require that the data processor run off a list of children with chronic attendance issues, which will be sent to the Counseling Office each week. Either way, it may be part of your job to make contact with the parent, send a series of attendance letters, or set up a parent conference with the parent and child to discover the cause for his excessive absences.

If there is documentation from a doctor or another medical professional, the issue is usually solved. If you find, however, that the child will be having numerous absences due to an ongoing medical problem, you should set up a meeting with the parent, child, all teachers involved, and an administrator. In this way, everyone will be informed and expect the absences and can prepare for them. I would also inform the school's Attendance Secretary and the Office of Attendance for the school system about the issue, so that the parents won't receive letters that they are in defiance of any mandatory state attendance law.

If you have a child who just misses time because he doesn't feel like coming to school, and the parents don't enforce his attendance, set up a conference in your office with the parent, child, and if you feel it is necessary, an administrator and discuss the ramifications to both the parent and child if he does not attend school. Have a copy of the attendance law for your state to hand to the parent and explain that parents can be charged, taken to court, and sometimes fined (depending on your state law) if their child doesn't attend.

Only present the copy of the law to the parent after you have tried to discover why the child is not coming to school. It may not be just laziness. The child may be a victim of a bully or may be avoiding class because he feels like he is failing no matter how hard he tries. If this is so, check the permanent record and see if the child needs a different placement. I also found more than once that a child missed school because he had to stay home and take care of younger siblings. You would be surprised what you can find out when you "look behind the curtain."

Even if you are dealing with a parent and/or child with a negative attitude, present the copy of the attendance law in a matter-of-fact, non-judgmental way. It should never be a threat—just a fact. Document that they received a copy, though (get them to sign, initial, and date one copy and place it in the child's file) so if the County/City Attendance Office contacts you, you have all of the required paperwork should the school system decide to prosecute the parent. Although the Attendance Officer of the school system may have the parent sign a duplicate copy at a later date if the attendance issue persists, your documentation from your parent/child meeting will be an important link in the chain to show that the parent was duly warned and had a chance to correct the problem.

*Private School, Home School Transfers, and New Students- Out of the many topics that I could have chosen for this chapter, I felt it was extremely important to mention these categories of new students. As far as private school and homeschooled children are concerned (we have already discussed ESL students), these children are suddenly dropped into a public school situation, sometimes for the first time, and can go through a genuine culture shock. For one thing, children from a private school are used to an overall smaller school environment with much smaller class sizes and usually much stricter rules in comparison with those in public education. On the other hand, homeschooled kids are used to a class of one or maybe participated in a small group and were directed by parent rules.

Walking down a crowded hall and seeing all kinds of behavior, as well as hearing some unmentionable words, can truly overwhelm these kids until they adjust. I have had more than one child come into my office with that "deer in the headlight" look. I have also had some appear at my office door with tears in their eyes. It can be quite an overwhelming experience at first.

Even if these categories of kids don't come looking for you, call them in for a conference after their first few days and check on how they are progressing. They may not be aware that they can come to see you. Let them know that you are there and ask them how things are going. They may talk, and they may not. If they will talk, ask them how they feel about moving from a smaller to a much larger situation. Asking them to compare the two will give you a clear picture of how they are adjusting, not only through their words, but by their facial expressions. At least they know that you are approachable if they have a problem. Remember your foreign exchange students, too.

Now in reference to new students, having been the new kid on the block several times during my school career (from public school to public school), I wish that my school counselor had taken the time to walk me around (it just takes a few minutes) and introduce me to my teachers before the school day started. I hated to just appear at the teachers' doors and ask if I were in the right place. The whole class gives you that group stare, and you feel like you are being immediately dissected.

Because I understand that feeling, I always gave the new student the *grande tour* of the building, at least pointing in the direction of the cafeteria, gym, library, and clinic, before I introduced him to his teachers, even if it took up a few minutes of homeroom or first period. I then walked the child back to first period class and introduced him to the class and asked who had the same second period as this student, thereby drafting his first buddy of the day. I also told the class which lunch the student had, and I always seemed to find a few kids who were pretty good about saying, "I have that class, too," or "I have that lunch."

Doing this can take a lot of stress off of the new student, even if he feels a little uncomfortable in the limelight. He's going to be in the limelight anyway when he walks through the classroom door, so you may as well use that awkward moment to help him feel that he is not so totally alone. First days can be the worst. I remember.

Of course, if you have some lead time because the student won't be attending school on the day that you enroll him, always email or drop a note in each teacher's box informing them about their new student and if the child has any special circumstances, such as the child is transferring from a private school, part of a military family returning from overseas, needs to sit in the front of the room due to eyesight or hearing issues, etc. Then they can prepare for the student, including making sure that they have an available desk for him, so there will be less disruption of class time all around when he walks through the door. Teachers really appreciate being alerted, and it gives you the opportunity to ask them to try to buddy up the child with someone from each class that day so you don't have to do this yourself. The teachers know who will make the best buddies and will be willing to help the new student find his way.

*Teaching Organizational Skills- Having been both a teacher and counselor, I have come into contact with some pretty scary lockers. Take a morning stroll through the halls before school begins, and it will change your perspective on the laws of three dimensional space. However, I warn you. Stand back! There will be some lockers that will explode upon opening. Books, notebooks, stray papers, pens, pencils, old tennis shoes, magazines, and an unknown substance that probably had once been a piece of fruit will come spewing out the minute the combination lock clicks on its last digit. I have seen lockers that literally were piled from the bottom up to eye level with stuff crammed sideways and in every nook and cranny. I kid you not. The loose papers themselves can take up half of the geometric space.

Backpacks can be miniature containers of horror, too. Wait until you see one that, once the zipper can be coerced to unzip, flowers into a shrub because the loose papers are trying to escape. *Disorganized* is a kind word to describe the owners of these compartments.

On the serious side, though, these are often right-brained, creative kids who just don't want to take the time to keep their "ducks in a row." Bless their hearts, some of them don't even seem to know where their ducks are!

Although we can't change personality and brain function, we can, as counselors, teach positive habits, one of which is how to get this kind of kid to stay at least somewhat organized because many of these kids are bright and do their homework. They just can't find it or end up grabbing the wrong book or notebook out of their locker as they hurry to class. Here are some suggestions to give these students, and don't forget to check behind them in the beginning to see if they are following through with the plan.

Skill 1- The backpack should be a portable locker and be carried to class with the student. At the beginning of each school day, all books and notebooks should be in the bottom of the locker, books on the bottom of the pile and notebooks together on the top of the books. The backpack should be empty, except for the book(s) or notebook(s) for the first class (or several classes, depending on when the child can return to his locker next).

Skill 2- Cover each textbook in a different color book cover and buy the same color notebook or folder to match the textbook. It solves the problem of grabbing the wrong book and notebook when a student is in a hurry between classes.

Skill 3- If the teacher gives the student a choice, have him get a folder of the same color in which notebook paper can be added and there is a pocket on one side to slip in tests, worksheets, and other important papers *temporarily* until he can punch three holes and insert them (hopefully!) when he gets home that night. Spiral notebooks tend to become emaciated really quickly because pages are constantly torn out for quizzes, tests, and writing notes to classmates. Then the student has to have more than one notebook for the same class. Overall, I found that slim, color-coordinated folders and three-ring binders are more efficient for this sort of child.

Skill 4- Each time the child returns to his locker during the day, he should place the books that he doesn't need to take home back into the bottom part of his locker and those books and notebooks that he will need to take in the top portion, which usually clicks open with a latch. If the student doesn't have a two-part locker, the student should turn a book sideways so that he will know that all books and notebooks above that visual marker need to be taken home. He can always leave the books that he will need in his backpack (if there is room), returning the ones not needed into the bottom of his locker.

Skill 5- In many schools the students are required to carry a school agenda in which the student is to keep a written list of daily homework assignments and dates for quizzes, tests, and projects. They are wonderful organizers, except for this type of child who already leaves other books and notebooks in his locker or at home on the floor of his room. Suggest that he learn to write his assignments in the agenda (the teacher may require it) but tell him as a back-up to always write the assignment in the top margin of the very next page in that class's notebook. Then when he grabs the correct book and notebook by color to take home but forgets his agenda, the assignment will be written on the top of the next blank page in that notebook, which is the one he should be writing his assignment on that very night.

And finally,

Skill 6- Tell the student to *never, never, never* dump out his entire backpack on his bed or the floor of his room (maybe on the kitchen table once in awhile to see what is growing in the bottom!). I had a parent come in one time with a stack of old homework assignments, signed tests, and papers that were completed but never turned in because the child dumped his backpack every night and papers by the droves had slipped behind and under his bed for months. The child had done the work, but those papers just never had a chance to make it back to school, and a teacher cannot grade what she cannot see. The papers existed but were missing in action, so that didn't help the child's grade at all. The key to dealing with this problem is to tell the student that he must teach himself that only one book and one notebook can sneak out of his backpack at a time, and they must be directly returned to the backpack before the next pair can escape from the pack. And if by chance you should have a child who forgets the whole backpack at home, tell him to put his shoes on top of it when he is done (he won't leave without them), or if it is a girl, put her purse on top of it. Need I say more?

Getting a student to make even some of these changes can really make a difference in a child's organization. It only takes a few weeks to create a habit that can over time become a lifesaver for a student who just doesn't know how to pull in his scattered energies. I had great success with these few strategies. It is particularly helpful on the middle and high school levels, but organizational skills should begin on the elementary level.

*Children Who Consistently Sleep in Class- There can be numerous reasons why a child consistently sleeps in class. None of them are good. I have had children who are bored and withdraw; children who wait until their parents are asleep and get back up to watch television, play video games, text, talk on their cell phone, or stay on the computer late into the night; children who end up having health issues; and children who have had their share of failure in school and are just afraid to try anymore. Whatever the issue, it is imperative that you call in the student and have a conference with the parent after a teacher has informed you of an ongoing problem.

Rooting out the reason may or may not be easy. If the child is just bored, check her records and teacher reports to see if she has been misplaced in a class and perhaps make a level change. In some cases, parents will end up having a heart-to-heart conversation with their kids and the TV, computer, etc. disappear from their room. Some parents end up taking their child to the doctor just to rule out a physical problem.

Then you have the child who has a history of failing or just feels so lost in a particular subject area that it's easier to withdraw and sleep than to try and continue to fail. Discovering that this is the problem can make all of the difference in whether or not that particular child will have a positive experience in school that year.

Having a parent conference, which includes the parent, the child, and the teacher(s) will make everyone aware of the desperation and feeling of hopelessness of the child, and proper measures can be taken to help her become successful. Even though the child may have built up a certain amount of resistance by then, that resistance can be whittled down over time if all parties are aware and work together for the benefit of the child. No child truly wants to fail, and when this student has had a few successes, what could have been a lost situation can be turned around.

*Children Who Fail on Purpose- Believe it or not, I sometimes ran into a kid who decided to fail on purpose. In every case that I encountered, all of these children could have passed and most of them, easily. So, why would a child purposely choose to fail, you might ask? Let me tell you only a few of the reasons that I discovered.

From all levels of school, I have had parent conferences with children who were terrified about transitioning from elementary school to middle school or from middle school to high school. On occasion, I even had rising ninth grade boys that were brought into my office crying because they were afraid to enter high school. Whether the parents had sent either overt or *meta-messages* to their child instilling them with fear of the change, or whether or not older siblings were trying to mess with their younger sibling's mind, the damage had been done, and that child's grades would begin to plummet as the end of the school year was growing closer and closer.

I found that the best way to deal with the fears of these children was to take them on the tour of the school and show them where everything is and how to work their locker. You would be surprised that one of their biggest fears is that their locker will get jammed, and they will be late to class and get marked tardy. It may seem like a small thing, perhaps, but it is *so* big to them.

School systems usually provide a school orientation for the rising classes, but some children need the assurance of one-on-one contact with a counselor just to know that there is someone they can run to if the locker gets jammed or if they get lost amid the crowded halls. Take the time to do this. In this case, *familiarity breeds contentment.*

In another case, I had a child who was extremely bright but had such a demanding and controlling parent that she felt that the only control she had was over her grades, so every other grading period, she would fail. Therefore, her overall average was a "C" or "D." I am not kidding! She told me that's why she did it. It drove her mom absolutely crazy, and it was her form of payback. I can't say that I was totally successful with this one. The issues between parent and child were long-standing and deep. However, I continued to try to impress upon the child that although she may be succeeding in driving her mother up the wall, she was damaging herself by building a roadblock between herself and her future plans for continuing her education after high school. Not only the grades, but the inconsistencies in her transcript would project a person who was not consistent or dependable in her work. Things did get better as the child matured, but some of the damage had already been done.

In one last case, I had a child who was terrified of graduating high school. He was an average student grade-wise, and although we had had conferences over the years and discussed possible careers of interest, he was still floundering.

If you think about it, in some ways graduating can be scary. I had kids who had already been accepted to a college tell me how scary the prospect of graduating was for them, so think about a kid who really can't seem to find a direction in which to move. For thirteen years (K-12th. grade), these kids have known where they would be every fall—back in school. Making the grand leap into life is a great unknown for them, no matter what they have planned. Therefore, some kids begin to fail during second semester.

When you see a child's grades suddenly plummet, call him in immediately and try to get a parent to come in, as well. What often helps is when a sympathetic parent or parents assure their child that Mom and/or Dad will be there to help them through this life change, and everything will be okay.

I am not talking about what we call "senioritis" among some high school students who think that they are "done with high school" and get lazy during second semester. Just remind these kids that their complete permanent transcript will be sent at the end of the school year to their college or prospective employer. That usually works. Colleges can and have withdrawn their initial offer of acceptance if a child's grades go down. Tell the kids this.

On extremely rare occasions, I did have kids who were told that when they graduated (turned eighteen), they were on their own, so they had better have a plan. Yep! One already had the kid's suitcases packed and waiting outside. I had another parent actually change the locks on the house doors.

It's probably a good thing that I won't say what I'm thinking right now, but you can imagine. However, these kids tended to know from their upbringing, or lack thereof, that this was the parent's expectation, and so they tended to have made plans to share an apartment with one or more friends or perhaps join the military, but not always. Remember that you can direct these kids to Adult Social Services if they have nowhere to go.

Anyway, when children begin failing for whatever reason, *conference, conference, conference.*

Social Issues

*Children Who Lack the Social Skills to Make Friends or Deal with Rejection-
No matter how much a child may protest, everyone deep down inside wants to make friends and be accepted. Rejection is something that no one seeks but is likely to experience at some point due to the demanding and incessant peer pressure that is the daily life's blood of the school environment.

As with adults, how a child will respond or recover from being rejected depends on his self-esteem, his personality, and his coping skills. Although a counselor cannot change the chemical or emotional predisposition of a child, she can teach coping skills to the student who just doesn't know how to respond in a group situation or is just too shy to initiate a conversation.

To a certain extent, you will have to base your counseling strategy on your assessment of each individual child's needs according to your observations of his personality and mindset. Obviously, what works for one child may be totally different from what another child may need. Getting the child to open up about how he feels or responds to others, both individually or in a group, will give you insight into his personality.

In a lot of cases, I found that the child was shy and lacked self-confidence. If someone spoke to him, he looked down and either responded with one word or not at all. This is a good opportunity to explore with this child what it would feel like if he were the person on the receiving end of his silence. Would he feel embarrassed by the lack of response? Would it be likely that he would want to attempt to strike up a conversation again with a person who appeared to totally dismiss him? Might he interpret the other person's lack of response as rudeness or perhaps snobbery? Might the other person feel rejected, too?

There are many approaches that you can take with this, but trying to get the child to understand how someone can misinterpret his shyness for any of the above interpretations seemed to be a strategy that worked for me.

I also used the age-old adage that in order to have a friend, you have to be one. I encouraged the child to work hard to overcome his shyness and some-times to be the first one to say "Hello." If the person doesn't respond back, it is a reflection on that person, not on him, and he should try not to interpret it as a form of rejection. There are rude and snobby people in the world, but they are not the ones he is seeking out to become his friends.

The key is to move on, and he is likely to find that he opens the door to make a friendship with another shy child because he can identify with those feelings. The child needs to understand that he has to send out a signal to others that he is accessible to them, or they won't take the time to try to get to know him if he chooses to hide himself behind a locked door. Teaching self-awareness, being aware of the feelings of others, and building coping skills will be your strongest strategies for helping a child in this kind of situation.

*Kids Who Crave Attention- The child who craves attention can appear in many disguises. It might be the girl who is waiting outside of your office every morning to see you before the day even begins. It might be the boy who watches for the days when you have Hall Duty so he can stand there and chat constantly about what happened yesterday or maybe give you a line by line summary of the book that he is currently reading (which is the third book in a trilogy which he will also tell you about). It could also be the overly dramatic extraverted girl who calls out your name loudly and throws her arms around you to give you a big hug in front of everyone else in the hall. I could go on and on.

Truthfully, I always found these kids to be very sweet but usually very needy, and the last thing you want to do is to hurt their feelings. How you decide to respond to their constant need for attention is really a judgment call on your part. Some counselors decide to take it in stride and accept them as a part of the day's routine so long as they aren't arriving late or missing class. Other counselors feel that to do so is a form of enabling.

I really don't want to give my opinion on what course to take here. Only you can decide by observation whether you are dealing with a fragile child or one who may love to always make herself the center of attention. My only advice is to tread gently on the feelings of the child when you have made your decision.

*Kids and the Dangers of the Web- Having been born one year after the invention of the television and at a time when a single computer was the size of a small warehouse, I have lived long enough to witness the onslaught of technology that far exceeds the excitement that I used to feel when I watched the futuristic technology of *Star Trek* in the 1960's. What used to be just a cell phone is now a multi-task gadget that rivals Captain Kirk's communicator, lacking the app, of course, of "Beam me up, Scottie."

Through desktop computers and hand-held cell phones that now connect directly to the Internet, our children have been given access to a world that we could only dream of. Forty years ago this concept was science fiction. Today this kind of access is taken for granted because today's children have never lived in a time without computers. It is both a blessing and a curse.

From a research point of view, it is a blessing for not having to sit in a library using books, periodicals, and encyclopedias that are not up to date or cannot be checked out, or perhaps waiting for weeks for someone to return the only copy of a book that you desperately need to complete your paper. We older folks have all been there.

But then enters the dark side of the internet. We all get sent or discover a lot of misinformation. Although this can be costly and aggravating, most of the damage can be corrected. However, the rise of Chat Rooms and other sites that are created to victimize children, who cannot see the people with whom they are communicating, has lead to horror stories that I need not discuss here.

Twice during my career, I was confronted with children who were chatting with adults on the Internet. These brazen men did not even pretend to be other teenagers, which, as you know, is quite prevalent among child predators. One was a man in his twenties who was communicating with one of my female counselees who was barely fourteen, and the other was an older man who was preying upon one of my boys whose single parent worked the nightshift, so the boy was not being supervised during that time.

It was sheer luck that I found out about both situations. A friend of the girl was so frantic that she stopped me in the hall to tell me that my counselee was making plans to meet with her contact and that begging her not to hadn't changed her friend's mind. In the case of the boy, he told me himself about the nice man who listened to his problems online and would like to meet him and take him out for dinner sometime.

On both occasions, I immediately called in each student that day and had a discussion about their online "friend." In the first case, I informed the girl, without revealing the source, that information had come to me about her possibly chatting online with an older man who wanted to meet her. She was resentful and angry but did not deny it had happened. Her ego had been boosted by the fact that a guy in his twenties showed interest in her (who knows how old he really was). Trying to convince her of the danger went in one ear and out the other.

While she sat there stewing as I explained what "Duty to Warn" means, I called her parent even before the chills stopped running up and down my own spine. Even if the child had denied it, I still would have been duty bound to warn the parent that the possibility might exist, and she might want to ascertain if this information were indeed true, as well as monitor her daughter's contacts. This particular child got a dose of how scared her parents were. They freaked and responded by removing the only computer that they had completely out of the house. If or when the computer was returned home, I never found out.

Following the same procedure in the case of the boy, he admitted that he was lonely, and this man acted like a father towards him. The parent's response in this case was to immediately take the computer keyboard and access cord and keep it under lock and key when he wasn't home to monitor his child.

There are as many reasons for a child to look for friendship on the Internet as there are predators who can reel in an emotionally needy or fearless child. As a counselor, you can only hope that these naïve kids aren't good at keeping secrets and will open their mouths to *someone*, whether it be to you, a teacher, or a friend who cares enough to possibly sacrifice a friendship for the safety of a friend.

Sometimes school systems will have assemblies where they have an officer of the law talk to the students about the dangers of the Internet. If not, it may be worth pursuing with your principal or with your colleagues about possible classroom presentations. However, always get approval by administration before you try to implement such a program because there may be a chance that some parent somewhere complains that the school has unnecessarily terrified her child. The main thing is that you should never hesitate to contact the parent the second you suspect a counselee may have made a dangerous online contact.

*<u>Broken Hearts and Hurt Feelings</u>- Whether it is Puppy Love or a child's first serious romance, having a broken heart is perhaps the worst experience that a child has had to endure so far in her life, unless it is the loss of a loved one or a pet. The loss of love hurts at any age, and we all know it. Overall, time and gaining perspective of the situation are the two great healers with this kind of pain.

Unfortunately, parents too often downplay a child's feelings with the remark, "You're young. You'll get over it. It wasn't serious anyway." It is usually because they don't want to, or don't know how to, deal with this kind of painful situation. How soon they forget!

On the other hand, they may instead hover over the child and inadvertently keep the child wallowing in self-pity. The truth is that it is serious to the child because she hasn't lived long enough to have developed a base of experience to put into context this heartbreaking event. All we have to do is look at Romeo and Juliet to realize how being young and lacking experience and perspective can have disastrous results. Youth is impulsive and reacts instantaneously to painful emotions, sometimes leaping to the notion that life is over. Combine this with feelings of self-doubt, humiliation (breakups communicated by texting, for instance), loss of status, anger, and betrayal, and we have a recipe brewing for possible depression, self-destructive behavior, or, in rare cases, thoughts of suicide. A lot will depend on the age of the child, as well as the personality and coping skills of that individual.

In my experience I found that most kids come to terms eventually with what has happened and move on. You as a counselor can fill an important role in the healing process because you are the objective outsider for them. You also care and are a non-judgmental safe haven for the child's feelings. As in any grieving process, getting the student to talk and explain the situation and what emotions that she or he is currently feeling (the emotions will fluctuate back and forth over time during this healing process) will force a form of self-talk as the child tries to explain or rationalize what has happened.

Between talking with you, their friends, and maybe their parents, children will eventually work through and assimilate what has happened to them. However, if at any time you feel that the child is depressed or worse, contact the parents right away and make them aware that the child may be at risk for destructive behavior. Never take any negative remark for granted because of the impulsive nature of young people. It is always better to be safe than sorry.

*Developmental and Maturity Factors- One of the things that can influence the outcome of a counseling session with a child is your ability to recognize and take into consideration the developmental and maturity levels of that individual.

Although personality and emotional construct will play a large part in a child's reaction to a particular issue or situation, his developmental and maturity level will influence how he comes to understand his options to resolve the problem or the consequences he must accept because of his actions.

It is up to you as his counselor to discover how to speak to a child in terms that he can understand and use examples that are concrete and clear enough when you are trying to help him decide how best to handle the situation. If you don't, it will be like trying to teach calculus to a first grader. His brain cannot grasp the concepts that you are using because he doesn't have the doorways of understanding open yet, and he has no context in which to place the examples you are giving him. When his eyebrows scrunch together or his eyes take on a glazed look, you will need to bring it down a notch and make your examples more concrete.

Although teaching abstract ideas (why he shouldn't lie, steal, or cheat, etc.) will become a common issue in your office, teaching him to recognize the impact that his choice has had on him and the others around him will need examples that the child can relate to and hopefully empathize with. For example, if a child is in your office for stealing a CD out of someone else's backpack, ask him the question, "John, do you have a favorite CD?" After he answers say, "Suppose you have it sitting on your desk and a person in class sees it and says, 'Wow, I love this CD. Thanks !' and then walks away with it. How would you feel?" After his answer, which is hopefully one that shows he has connected with the concept, ask, "How do you think the boy whose CD you took felt when you did that to him?"

This is what I mean by using a concrete example so that the child can hopefully understand the feelings of the other person who was affected by his actions. To just say that stealing is wrong won't impact this child because knowing that it is wrong didn't stop him from stealing in the first place. He needs to make a lasting connection to begin to assimilate the higher concept that stealing will hurt him and other people.

Spend some time formulating a series of good concrete examples and strategies that are age-based to use in these situations ahead of time so that you will have ready access to them when any moral issue comes in your door.

*__Peer Pressure__- I would imagine that most of us would agree that the major culprit influencing children to make a multitude of mistakes during their youth is peer pressure. Everyone has experienced it. Adults do, too. The difference is that when adults give in to peer pressure, they should have had enough life experience and self-confidence to know better. Children usually don't have either of these things. All they want is to be accepted and sometimes accepted at any cost.

If you are currently, or have ever been, a parent at any time in your life (You finally raised them!), you may have had a temporary bald spot at some time or another from ripping your hair out or discovered that you had gotten a little gray around the temples before it was through. Kids can float blissfully down the river without a paddle and have no clue that they are heading for a set of rapids that could rip their boat apart, while we as parents are standing on the shore screaming to watch out for the danger, which sometimes might permanently damage their life.

I feel for the child in his ignorance, but I also feel greatly for the parent. You will probably get as many frustrated and scared parents in your office as you will get their kids who have that special arrogance of youth on their side. Teenagers, in particular, live in a transitory state where currently their number one concept is that adults are stupid and don't understand anything.

When the parent asks you to call her child in and talk to him, expect the height of resistance and resentment towards you and the parent or adult who let you in on the not-so-smart choices that this child has been making in his life. It will be up to you to break down that resistance in the same way you would with any child: non-judgment, attention to details (make him give you as many details about what is going on as you can squeeze out of him), logical and concrete examples of possible consequences and alternate choices, and a great deal of patience on your part.

Check in with him at regular intervals for awhile, and make it clear to the parents that you will continue to be a sounding board but that you have limitations as to how much you may be able to influence the child's choices. Reiterate to the parents that spending time and creating an atmosphere at home where their child feels that he can comfortably talk with them about what is going on in his life is their best chance to become aware and intervene in any situation that they deem dangerous.

One tenant of good parenting is for them to be able to put on their invisible suit of armor in preparation for a possible nasty battle, tether their emotions to the nearest hitching post, face their child and say the one word no kid wants to hear, "NO." It's okay if their kid doesn't like them for awhile. It may hurt, but they have the ultimate responsibility to use their best judgment and try to keep their child out (or pull him out) of the harrowing rapids of his negative choices. They are not their child's *friend* but their *parents,* and it can be tough.

You can be a support to the child and the parents by your role as an objective outsider, and having a conference with the parents and child can be very beneficial because you may be able to mediate any bad feelings. However, be very careful not to cross the line into individual or family therapy. Dealing with peer pressure is tough for everyone, but you can possibly be a positive influence in the life of the parent and child by viewing the situation from a global and less personal perspective.

Behavioral Issues

*__Bullying__- The issue of bullying has now gained nationwide recognition, not only because of traditional bullying, but also for the devastating and sometimes tragic results that have happened due to *cyber-bullying*. The ramifications of bullying, both physically and emotionally, are so serious and so extensive that there is no way that I can adequately cover a subject that is being addressed in full length books.

To be sure, bullying is an issue that will darken your door incessantly, and it is imperative that you understand the attitude and requirements of your school system and your school administrators. You also need to be cognizant of your own personal feelings regarding bullies, particularly if you experienced being bullied at anytime in your formative years. You don't want your "old dirt" to slip through when you are working with either a bully or the victim of a bully. The damage a bully can do can influence someone's emotions for a lifetime, and you are no exception to the rule. Acknowledge and own those feelings but recognize that they have no place in the current situation, except understanding that the bully, as well as the victim, is a damaged child.

This epiphany came to me one day when I was speaking to a middle school class about academic, as well as social issues. In my effort to cover the subject of both the bully and the victim without trying to sound judgmental, I asked the question, "Where do you think people learn to bully?" Well, in doing so, I unexpectedly opened a "can of worms" because I was thinking from an adult perspective and thought that I would hear a kid give an expected answer, such as from a sibling, on the playground, or in sports. Instead, the very first answer that came out of the first student's mouth was spoken by a known bully who answered, "Your parents." For a split second, I was really taken aback, not only by the response but by the child who had spoken it.

I learned several valuable lessons that day. You need to anticipate as many possible responses to any question that you are going to ask to children because they can be more insightful and deadly honest than you think. Although it may be difficult to swallow when bullies can be so cruel, remember that they are children who are victims, too, and their way of dealing with it is to victimize others before someone can victimize them (again).

Above all, when you become aware of a child who is being bullied, deal with it immediately. Don't let it continue for a moment. Some children are not emotionally strong enough or intellectually capable of putting into action advice that you may give them on how to deal with the bully the next time. Call for a mediation between the bully and victim immediately. This lets the bully know that you are on to him. If that doesn't work, involve administration and the parents, if needed.

If the situation has to become a discipline problem because all else fails, remember that you cannot instantly undo the learned negative behavior of the bully, nor the hurt feelings of the victim. Sometimes it takes discipline by an administrator to send the message to both the bully and his parents that this type of behavior is not a child's rites of passage and that **bullying will not be tolerated under any circumstances.**

Hopefully, your school system has or will instigate a Bullying Initiative, and you, as well as the teachers, will be called upon to educate all children that self-respect and respect for others is a part of one's integrity for a lifetime and that there will be consequences for their actions if they have difficulty learning this concept.

*Dealing with the "Rumor Mill"- "Well, Mrs. Di Peppe. This is how it all started. *They* said that *she* said that *he* said that…Then *I* said that *they* were wrong and that *he* had said what *she* had said that… Then *she* heard what *I* had said and that's when *she* came looking for *me* at lunch to fight *me*."

Ah, the "Rumor Mill." Sometimes it seems that it is part of the fiber optics of the social network in a school. It also loops you in by making you the logical sounding board to validate everyone's point of view when it rears its ugly head once again to prey on its next victim. Reputations have been raised up or destroyed by its very existence.

Your office will become a makeshift shelter for the eventual fallout for its creators and/or victims, depending on who shows up at your door first. In some cases, you will have at least one of the culprits show up and swear that she never said such a thing and was being falsely accused and now everyone is mad at her. Then, at other times, the victim of spiteful gossip will end up coming to your office truly devastated by what is being said about her. At other times an administrator will have gotten wind of what is going on and will send the involved parties to your office before the problem escalates into a fight. Obviously, in all cases, mediation is the Word of the Day.

My first suggestion is to talk to whoever ends up in your office first so you have the basic storyline and cast of characters before you send for anyone else. By doing this, you can identify the major characters in the scenario because it is not always necessary to pull everyone in for a conference. Hold the mediation in a neutral room, like a conference room. Why? Well, obviously, one of the group is a counselee of yours, or they wouldn't have come to you. You don't want the other or others involved to think that you are automatically taking the side of your student.

I found that the way to quickly smother a rumor is to only bring in the initiator and the victim, and possibly the one with the biggest mouth who is spreading the rumor like wildfire. Make sure that you control the time frame of the mediation, or you could be there all day. These kinds of kids love to talk. Give each one her time to give a capsule summary of how this all began (no theatrics allowed, just facts) and quell any interruptions, reminding them that they will have their time to speak. Mediate their differences from the information that you obtain, but make it extremely clear that it all ends now and that they are to make it clear to their friends who have taken sides that the problem has been resolved, and the subject is closed. Rumors die a lonely death if they are not acknowledged, and they are all responsible for stopping the rumor mill. Otherwise, the consequences of their choices will be that the control will be taken out of their hands and given to an administrator because their actions are causing a disruption in school.

If you observe that any one of the children involved may still be looking for trouble, let the others go, talk with her, and if you still don't get any results, tell the child that you will be talking with a parent, or better yet, call the parent with the child still in your office. I rarely had to do this, but it is better than having the child leave your office and get into a fight. Parents want to know and have more power over their child than you do. Tongue in cheek, they can threaten their kid that they better not cause trouble that will get them suspended or force the parent to have to leave work and come to the school. Make it your last resort because you want to teach children the proper way of mediating disputes in an open and civil manner. Only involve a parent or administrator if you feel that a child is going to hurt another child or refuses to be mediated and the behavior continues.

*Inappropriate Social Behavior Between Male and Female Students- Love is always in the air when you are working in a school. Nature has an ace in her pocket, and the line between what is appropriate or inappropriate behavior grows fuzzy in the mind of the students. Hormones are dancing, and keeping an eye out for improper shows of affection becomes every administrator's headache.

I don't plan on giving any specific experiences from my career here, but suffice it to say that your imagination doesn't have to take you far to know that if you are in education long enough, you will probably encounter stories of some pretty steamy stuff before it is all said and done, barring the elementary level, of course. Luckily, any heavy duty incidents will probably bypass you and go straight to administration for possible school board action. What will usually end up in your office is the in between class "make-out session" behind the lockers or the blatant display of affection in the halls. It becomes somewhat of a battle because the kids are doing what kids do, and they will sit in your office and roll their eyes at you when you talk to them about what is appropriate and inappropriate behavior in a school setting. Expect an attitude of "Big deal" or "They're an adult and don't understand" to be written all over their faces.

How you handle this situation, especially if it is ongoing with a couple, may vary according to your school's protocol. However, if you are used as the first line of defense, I suggest that you use a four-step approach (if possible) if the behavior doesn't stop: 1) Conference in your office with both kids. 2) Inform a parent of their continued breaking of the school rules. 3) Have a conference with each child and a parent in your office and discuss possible ramifications for ignoring the rules. 4) Now, it is an administrative problem.

If the administrator suspends the kids until parents bring them back to school for a parent conference, ask if the administrator wants you to be part of the conference, since you have already dealt with the situation three times by then. Keep good notes and any dates of your conferences and phone calls.

Don't be surprised at the many and varied reactions you will get from parents regarding their child's behavior. Some will take care of the problem immediately because they are embarrassed, some will think it's funny and not take it seriously, some will get angry and think that the school is making a big deal out of nothing or is perhaps picking on their kid, and some will tell you what they think you want to hear and do nothing about it.

At this point, the chronic behavior has become a discipline problem, and you may not have any influence in the matter, unless the administrator chooses to include you. I have had both happen during my career, and it will often be the domain of the administrator to make the decision in ongoing behavioral issues.

*Lying, Cheating (Honor Code Violation), or Stealing- Although we are considered in *loco parentis* (in place of the parent) when a child is in school, teaching morality to a child on a fundamental level is, and always has been, the responsibility of the parent. Children are raised by people who have their own measuring stick for what is right or wrong, and it doesn't always match the expectations of what society mandates.

Unfortunately, some children are taught to do whatever it takes to get what they want so long as they don't get caught. As an example, I once met with a counselee in my office who had returned from being suspended for fighting in school. He didn't seem to be remorseful or open to mediation, nor did he respond to the negative consequences of being suspended. So, as a logical question, I asked him how his parents had reacted to his trying to solve the issue through fighting, and his words in response were unemotional and very straightforward, "They just told me to wait next time until I got off the bus in the afternoon to fight."

As a counselor, how do you respond to this? It is the task of the parents to lay the foundation of acceptable moral conduct for their child, and you can't disparage them in front of the child, no matter how much you may disagree with them. The only way I found to deal with this type of situation, no matter what moral issue it involves, is to make a distinction between an individual family's expectations and those of institutions outside of his personal sphere. Society has laid down rules and laws for the general benefit and protection of all of its citizens, whether it is for a school, the workplace, or in the public domain. We must accept and adapt to these established laws or the consequences will be taken out of our hands, and the punishment can be so severe that an individual could lose his freedom. This is the reality of our choices.

Even if you get an expression from the child that includes a rolling of his eyes, you have not failed. All you can do is plant the seed of what society mandates as acceptable and lawful behavior and hope that it takes root. With the help of time and maturity and perhaps enough negative consequences (learning the hard way, hopefully while he is still a child), he finds that it just isn't worth his wile to continue in his chosen behavior.

*Disrespectful Behavior Towards Teachers- Having been a classroom teacher for half of my career, I know a lot about this kind of behavior. Whether you as a counselor see the child before or after he has been sent to an administrator is usually the result of the tolerance level of the teacher and sometimes the frustration level of the parent.

Depending on the mindset of the teacher or the administrator, or maybe the desperation of the parent who is tired of getting phone calls at work or home regarding the insolence of her child, one way or another, you will probably meet with at least some of these little darlings who just don't seem to understand where the line is drawn between interacting with an adult or interacting with their peers. Disrespectful behavior can be modeled at home, be a product of the personality construct of the child (I have met some really nice parents with some really hard-headed kids), or the result of a child who needs attention (negative attention can be better than no attention at all) and likes to show off in front of his peers. Whatever the reason, your task is to find out why the child just doesn't seem to "get it" and continues to sabotage himself.

One of the things to consider is whether or not the child is a discipline problem in just that one class or if he is an all-round pain in the posterior for some or all of his teachers. If the problem is with one teacher, he will usually tell you so, saying that teacher picks on him or isn't fair. The match between teacher and student is not always a perfect one and personalities will clash. However, the teacher has control of the class, and the child has to adapt to the expectations of the teacher, whether he likes it or not. The student needs to understand that in the future, he can't talk back or quit every job when he doesn't like his boss, or he will never be able to hold a job or get a positive recommendation. He will have to find a way to adjust and create a working relationship with the person who is writing his paycheck, or in this case, will be giving him a final grade because at this moment, school is his job.

On the other hand, if the child is an overall discipline problem, have a conference with all of his teachers in the same room and look for his patterns of behavior. They are the ones who see him on a daily basis and have the data you need through their observations and perspective in the classroom. Go back and review the child's permanent record and gain insight through his former teachers. From this research you will have a global view of the child's academic and behavioral progress throughout his school career, and you may even find that the behaviors didn't start until recently. Then again, you may find that the child has had difficulty in school from Day One. Looking at the cumulative record, meeting with the current teachers, and hopefully getting the parent's perspective will provide you with the background information that can give you your best chance at helping the child when you meet with him again (and again and again) in your efforts to make him self-aware and responsible for his own behavior.

Yes, it can be time-consuming, but I always asked teachers to call me with both negative and positive reports of the student's progress. A short checklist form for Weekly Observations with a space for Any Additional Remarks can also be created by you and dropped in the teachers' boxes. It doesn't take any time for them to check off their observations, and they really appreciate your support for tracking the student with them.

It is imperative that you demonstrate to the teachers, as well as parents, that you back up your words with action. You also owe it to the child to attempt to solve the problem, if possible, or at least encourage a change of behavior that will make his school experience have a more positive outcome.

*The "Sarah Bernhardt Effect" (aka, "the Drama Queen"- manipulation, not necessarily dysfunction)- I am not really a betting person, but by sheer numerical odds because of the number of counselees you will be assigned during any one school year, you will have at least one "Drama Queen" among the bunch. Before you jump to the conclusion that I am being unkind by putting a label on a child, please understand that I am fully aware that these children are in desperate need of attention from anyone and everyone who they can grab it from. That, in itself, is an indicator of what may be a much larger problem. It is that awareness on your part that gives you a springboard to work from with this child because you will definitely be seeing her a lot (I only had one "Drama King" in my career, but they do exist).

In retrospect, I think that Drama Queens can be subdivided into two types. The first type is a genuinely sincere child who can be a victim of her own personality construct or dysfunctional upbringing and can be very sensitive and unprepared to deal with any kind of situation when things don't go smoothly during the day. These children can be fragile and may need expert help in learning how to cope with the day-to-day stresses in their life. Remember, **you are not a therapist**, but you can talk to the school psychologist and scheduling a meeting with the parent may help in your understanding of the child. You may also find that the child is already getting outside counseling, and the parent may give you permission by a <u>Written Release of Information</u> form to talk with the child's therapist. One way or another, you are going to have to discover, if possible, what the underlying factors are that spawned this type of intense behavior before you can decide how to deal with it.

However, in the case of the self-made Drama Queen (Type 2), when this kind of behavior starts early in the school year, and a child is making a big deal out of nothing or everything, she is probably testing you to see how much time and sympathy that she can draw out of you before you become wise to her actions. It will only take a few times for you to realize that this girl is trying to manipulate you and take up a lot of your time for her own purposes, like missing quizzes or tests or not having her homework done. Check with her teachers and watch for a pattern. It will be there.

In addition, observe how this kind of Drama Queen tends to get her emotions under control just in time to go to lunch with her friends. In the meantime, you have been tied up in your office with contrived hysteria which can sometimes be turned off with the ringing of the bell for the next class, while there is another child who is waiting to see you who really needs help. When you have observed this child's pattern developing over a period of time, you will know how best to get her under control.

No matter what the scenario, it is important to set limits on her time with you. When she comes in hysterical with her problem of the week (or day), immediately take an offensive stance. Have her sit down, close the door so that she doesn't draw anymore attention to egg her on (she has probably already caused a scene in the Counseling Office by her dramatic entrance), tell her to take a deep breathe to calm herself, and then assure her that you both will deal with the problem. Ask her to describe the problem. If she starts to digress and go off on tangents that don't apply, immediately refocus her to the issue at hand. It shouldn't take long to get the gist of the problem. In a brief summary, repeat the issue back to her so she knows that you understand. Ask her what she thinks can be done to remedy the situation. Then give your input, and assure her that you believe in her ability to solve this situation and then send her back to class.

You will know immediately if you have caught her in the act of trying to get out of class or just take up your time if she gets that peeved look in her eye because she expected to stay in your office for a lot longer time. If she tries to start up the whole thing again, just stop her and remind her that she knows what she needs to do, and you know she can handle this. After awhile, the visits to your office should wane because she knows that you have figured out her game. Never allow these girls to have free rein on any given day. You remain the one in control.

If this isn't effective, you decide how best you should handle this. You may have to bring in a parent or an administrator if you have difficulty controlling her behavior. Also, don't forget to let the other counselors and the counseling secretary know who this child is so that she won't come looking for hours of attention if you are absent that day. Drama Queens can be very savvy because they have learned how to manipulate people from a young age.

Just as counselors usually make each other aware of at-risk children, in case they appear in the office on a day when their counselor is either absent or unavailable and will need to be seen by someone, let them know about those children, such as manipulative Drama Queens, who could take up their time unnecessarily when they need to be working on other issues.

Counselor Issues

*Get to Know Your Social Workers- Although I have spoken at length earlier in this chapter about calling Social Services, I would like to now stress the importance of building a relationship with your local social workers. Although a situation is out of your hands once you make a report to Child Protective Services, there may be numerous calls and visits to the school by the social worker who has been assigned the case in order to gain information from the child, from school records, and from you as the child's counselor. Not only are these people amazing individuals who deal with unthinkable situations of child abuse and domestic violence everyday and still do not lose faith in humanity, they can also be founts of information about the law, how to handle particular issues with the family who may have had a history with Social Services already, and can be a wonderful resource when you are unsure if you have enough grounds to make a report.

Sometimes when I was frustrated because I knew that I couldn't make a documented report on a child due to the lack of physical evidence (unfortunately, emotional abuse can be just as damaging but is extremely difficult to prosecute), I would call one of the several social workers who I had worked with for many years just to gain some kind of perspective on what I could do, if anything. For the child's sake and my own peace of mind, I wanted to make someone aware of my unease and that I felt that it was just a matter of time before my concerns might become provable. It was because we had nurtured a relationship over the years that I was always taken seriously, and even when a formal report could not be made, these dedicated workers were always there to be a sounding board for my concerns.

One of these wonderful ladies told me once that the attrition rate for the average social worker is three years. I was so lucky to have known four outstanding workers who had more than twenty years each under their belts and still had a sense of humor. Talk about amazing people!

My hope for you is that you don't have to make reports to Social Services that often, but when you do, please take the opportunity to get to know at least one social worker who you feel you can communicate with well, if possible. That person will be one of your most valuable assets for one of the most difficult duties in your job description. Because of these workers, I was able to sleep at night knowing that they were the sentinels at the gate.

*Keeping Counselor Records- Obviously, it is imperative that a counselor keep quality records, whether it is regarding a meeting with a counselee, a parent, a teacher or administrator, or for a parent-teacher conference. In some cases, only a few sentences may be needed to remind you of a task you must perform, such as calling in a child at the request of a teacher or an administrator. Unless it is required, it is not necessary that you keep a file on every single student assigned to you. In some instances, record keeping is often left to counselor preference. I suggest that you keep records that you feel you may need to reference in ongoing situations with parents or students or ones that you may need to protect yourself if you foresee a possible legal issue arising.

Your district will probably have its own requirement for what is considered *timely* in the purging of your records. I personally only kept counselor files on students who had specific or ongoing problems or special needs. However, it is for this reason that I want to caution you. Be very cognizant of what you write down and what observations that you make or conclusions that you may draw from a particular meeting. You may keep your files confidential, but remember that under the law, your files can be subpoenaed and what you choose to write down could come back to haunt you.

Rule of thumb: write down only what is said and what you observe. DON"T write down your speculations, such as, "I wonder if there has been child abuse in the family," or "I really think that this student should be medicated." Need I say more about how these kinds of comments can get you into a world of trouble if they are brought out in open court. What you may surmise and what is reality may be totally different, and, as always, I repeat, and will continue to repeat, *never, never* forget that you are **NOT** a therapist.

Keep these personal student files preferably in a locked cabinet in your office. I highly caution you to not take them out of the school building. If you lose one, such as dropping it in the parking lot, you don't want to even think of the ramifications. Counselor Calendars or Daybooks, such as the logs that I am using for this section of the book, should never include any personal information about what happened between you and your counselee or parent in your office. Logs are lists of daily appointments and duties that counselors carry with them, not personal records. Make very sure that you keep these two forms of documentation separate at all times.

*Homeless Children- Sadly, homelessness is a growing problem in our society. The number of these children who become your counselees will change from moment to moment. This is based on the fact that they may often have to change schools several times during the year, depending on whether they are living in a temporary shelter, a relative's home, or a temporary placement in a hotel room or apartment by Adult Social Services.

The one constant is that this is a heartbreaking situation for everyone involved. It is important to get to know these children and their parents so that you can find out their individual circumstances and needs. It is also important to meet with the teachers and disseminate whatever information that the parent will allow (if any) so that the teachers are aware that the child may have extra needs.

Children who are bounced around from place to place and school to school most often have gaps in their education, and what we may assume that they learned in an earlier grade may be missing in their actual skill level. Even if a child is homeless for the first time, it might be nearly impossible for a child to do her homework when she is sharing a single hotel room with her whole family, especially if there are younger siblings, such as a baby. All these issues need to be addressed when possible.

In addition, although Social Services tries to help, with the current economy and budgetary cut-backs, holidays, such as Christmas, can be difficult times for the homeless. One of the things that gave me the most satisfaction was when we, as a department, obtained information, such as the ages, clothes sizes, and even favorite colors of our homeless children and usually their siblings and collected gifts that either the parents came to pick up or we delivered to the families for the holidays. The children's names were always confidential, but the children's teachers usually knew about the circumstances because most of the children themselves did not keep their homelessness a secret. It was at those moments that I was reminded that the spirit of unselfish giving was alive and well. I witnessed the tremendous outpouring of generosity from the faculty and other school personnel as the wall of presents in the Counseling Office grew larger and larger each day.

You have an opportunity to become a link between school and home for this child so that she may have as much support as possible to keep her on track in her education. Checking in on a regular basis with the homeless child's teachers on her academic progress, as well as gaining insight from the teachers' ongoing observations of the behavior of the child in the classroom, will be your best asset in monitoring how the student is faring in one of the most difficult situations that a child can experience.

Note: it is imperative that you become knowledgeable of the McKinney-Vento Act, which was enacted on the federal level to protect homeless children.

*Homebound Children- Your initial thoughts about having to deal with a child who has been placed on Homebound Instruction (usually decided by a physician for medical reasons) is that this situation is pretty cut and dried. Just talk to the parent, get the documentation, send a group note or email to the child's teachers requesting the student's work for a specified number of days (often a week at a time if long term), and then speak with the homebound teacher to set a time for her to pick up the student's work and return it to be graded. I wish it were that simple. Sometimes it is.

Then there are those other times when you may feel that you are at the center of a three-ring circus. I don't say this to disparage anyone—not the student, the teachers, or the parents. It's just that everyone's expectations in a homebound situation can collide without warning. For instance, a teacher or teachers may complain that the work that has already been sent to the child was returned unfinished or poorly done, and they complain about the homebound teacher and resent having to prepare additional work when the assignments that they worked hard to prepare were sent back incomplete.

The homebound teacher may complain that the student was given some assignments that she was not prepared for and more background explanation was needed by the teacher before the child could attempt to complete the work. Therefore, the homebound teacher was left at odds with what to do with the student in that subject area, so she sent back the work incomplete asking for more explanation on the part of the teacher.

As this distressing back and forth game of 'homework badminton" rages on and on, the parent may then call you upset because he may feel that his child is beginning to fall behind in his schoolwork, or the child is getting back graded tests/assignments with an unacceptable grade (There really are some parents who think that their child should get all high grades while on homebound). The homebound teacher only visits a few hours per week, and parents need to understand that it is their responsibility to monitor their child's progress and make sure that the assignments are worked on consistently, even when the teacher is not present.

While homebound appears to be just an administrative task for you as a counselor, it really can at times become such a tangle. As with most things, communication is the key. What really helps is to try to set up a conference with the homebound teacher and all of the teachers at the onset and let them discuss the work and student/teacher expectations with one another. If possible, try to get the parent to attend so that he can get a clear picture of what can be expected from all parties involved. Parents are an integral part of the process and need to understand how important it is for them to participate in their child's homebound experience, as well. If they don't consistently check behind the child to make sure that she is completing the assigned work in between visits by the homebound teacher, then they really don't have much room to complain if the child gets less than spectacular grades (Of course, there will always be some who will complain, anyway). Homebound is a group effort and everyone has their part to play. Parents are no exception. They should not be allowed to delegate their responsibility in this matter to the homebound or regular teachers.

Overall, homebound usually progresses well, but if you do have a situation where some or all parties seem at odds, set up another meeting and sort it out. Use your diplomacy, and don't ever let anyone point a finger of blame at another. That serves no purpose and becomes a roadblock to the student's progress. Keep everyone from getting sidetracked and remind them that the focus is on making the child's experience a positive one while she is striving to get well and come back to school.

*<u>Helping Teachers with their Discipline Problems</u>- I always (and still do) have great empathy for a teacher who will swear to you that "Little Lucifer" sits in the second row and three seats back in her first period class. Even a veteran teacher can eventually be at her wits end when she has disciplined the student, called home for parental support, had a parent conference, and even referred the child to an administrator without seeing a positive change.

In many cases, a teacher will refer the child to you before writing a referral to an administrator, but not always. It really depends on whether or not the teacher takes you seriously as a resource. That is why building a positive relationship with teachers is so important, which I stressed earlier in this book. You are responsible for projecting your competence and accessibility as a valuable asset to the school. No one can do that for you. You don't want a teacher seeking you out for help only because the administrator won't deal with the child before the student has seen his counselor first. This means that you are viewed as only an intermediary and required step on the way to the administrator's office and not as a valuable link in the process of a child's education.

Luckily, I always found that a majority of teachers preferred to handle their own discipline problems within the framework of their classroom rules and structure, anyway. I did. So, keep in mind that if a teacher comes to you for help with a child who is a behavioral problem, especially, but not exclusively, a veteran teacher, you can bet that she has probably exhausted her options and is proactively seeking positive solutions because that child's disruptive behavior is affecting the education of the other students in the class.

At this point, go pull the child's general academic file and review it with the teacher, unless it is a policy in your school district that academic files, not just special education files, are confidential. A lot can be gleaned from a child's transcript of grades, test scores, and teacher observations that can show a pattern of the student's academic and behavioral progress.

Take good notes and ask for specific examples of the child's behavior. Also, ask what steps the teacher has taken already so you can quote these to the child or parent when you meet with them. In this way, you have undeniable proof that a problem exists, and it is not that "the teacher is just picking on me," or "picking on my child." The more examples you have, the better.

It is really up to you whether you decide to just meet with the child, meet with the child and teacher together, meet with the child and parent(s), or meet with the child, parent, and teacher. Any and all of these conferences are options and can be very beneficial. I usually began with a meeting just with the child, discussing each concern or problem that had been presented to me and giving the child an opportunity to be heard. Then if I found that she refused to take any personal responsibility for her actions, I would inform her that I would be calling to set up a conference with her, her parents, and the teacher because the next step would be a teacher referral to an administrator and would then be outside of my purview. In more cases than not, that usually worked, since most parents don't like being interrupted at work, and the child knows that it won't bode well for her when she gets home, even if the parent is on the defensive.

Discovering why the child is acting out in class is then left up to you by asking the right questions. Read between the lines of the child's complaints, and you will find the answers. Talk to her about each incident, ask her to tell you how she responded so she will have to hear herself trying to explain her actions to you, and then inquire how she might have handled the situation in a different way and how she can prevent it from happening again. Not only are you teaching the child self-awareness of her behavior and choices, but you are demonstrating that you are not being judgmental by asking *the child* to come up with *her* own solution to the problem.

By doing this, you are a counselor, not an administrator. You don't want the line to blur between these two job descriptions because we can all get "preachy" now and then. I had to catch myself plenty of times, particularly if I knew the child well. Give it your all but realize that some kids are bound for the administrator's office no matter what you do. Never give up on them but stay realistic and keep looking for any solutions that may help the child become more cognizant of her actions.

Finally, I would like to note that there were a few instances in my entire career that a teacher tried to hoodwink me into doing *her* discipline *for* her. Her pattern of behavior became apparent very quickly. Should you have this happen and you are unsure of what to do, speak to your director and gain some input before you decide how to handle this situation in a professional manner, not only for your own sake, but particularly for the child. To become a disciplinarian is a conflict of interest, and somehow you will have to find a way to diplomatically let this teacher know that this is not part of your job.

*Don't Make Promises that You Can't Keep- With your best intentions in tow, you may find that in the heat of the moment, you sometimes can make promises that you cannot keep. There you are, neck-deep in taking care of that day's issues with children, returning parent phone calls, fulfilling requests from teachers and administrators, and preparing for a parent conference. All of a sudden, another face appears at your door asking you to complete some task, find out some information, see another child, or call yet another parent not on your list before the day is through—the key words being in all of these cases, *before the day is through.* Instantly, you hear yourself saying out loud (before your overwhelmed brain has a chance to process that there already aren't enough hours in the day to complete everything you *already* have to do), "Sure. No problem." There you have it—an unconscious promise, and guess what? All your good intentions go to dust when a parent shows up unexpectedly at your office to see you, a crying child comes in the door, or an administrator calls you up to his office about one of your kids. The next thing you hear is the ringing of the bell that ends the school day.

No matter how meticulous and organized a person you may be, there will be days like this because of the amount of children you have in your caseload and the nature of your job. Most people will understand if you don't get their particular task done that day, but those who don't can be quite condescending and some of them downright ugly.

Towards the end of my career, this kind of momentary promise was still an occasional pitfall for me because I really wanted to help. However, in my more sane moments, I did imprint a specific line into my mainframe and, as time went on, remembered to spit it out at the appropriate moment: "I can't promise that I can get it done for you by the end of the day, but I will try. Otherwise, I will work on it tomorrow." That person may not be happy with the answer, but they need to understand that you cannot drop everything that you are already doing just to take care of his problem (unless it is an administrator who is demanding it *now,* and you have no choice).

It's okay to give yourself a temporary "out" because you can never predict what problem may be walking towards your office as we speak. You will always have to prioritize, and you have to survive and get the job done. So, be patient with yourself and others, but bite your tongue when it comes to making daily promises in your effort to please everyone. All your good intentions can backfire on you, and you have enough on your plate as it is.

Chapter 23: A Jack of All Trades, a Master of "Some"

"I do respect you. I also respect the janitor."

> Daniel Negreanu
> Professional Poker Player
> Las Vegas, Nevada

It is well-earned and well-deserved that you should be very proud of yourself for accomplishing your career goal, which was to become a counselor. In many states this requires a Master's degree, and the time, dedication, and hard work that it takes to achieve this status is over and beyond the level of education that most people pursue. Yet, it is about this idea of *status* that I feel the need to talk.

In some schools, counselors have to work hard to not be viewed as an isolated unit in the building. Neither "beast nor fowl", counselors can be easily stereotyped by those who don't really understand what a counselor does. Since you are neither a classroom teacher nor an administrator, there will be those who misjudge your role and believe that you have authority over them or get special treatment because you may not have to sit hall duty, cafeteria duty, or stay for some afternoon functions. You would be surprised how these slight differences can cause a fair share of antipathy among some and allow them to develop an erroneous mindset about who *they* think you are, what *they* think you do, and what *they* believe that you won't do. It is this preconceived mindset of some colleagues that you may need to break by demonstrating that you are an equal cog in the wheel that keeps the school running smoothly and that you are neither less than, nor more important than, any other cog. This may or may not be difficult, but it can certainly be achieved with effort on your part.

There are a myriad of ways to make yourself a part of the ongoing routine of the building. Granted, some of the things that I will mention may seem ludicrous to you because you are up to your eyelids with work already. I know that these are activities that you can't do everyday, but when you have the time, you should not be above offering to do some of these things. You are really no different than anyone else, but you may have to prove it by your actions if you ever want to be truly understood. If you stay in your office and have everyone come to you, you will never dispel the myth that school counselors think that they are "all that" and above doing certain tasks. You will also miss the wonderful interaction that you can have with all of the children and adults in the building.

Anyone in any job can have times when they feel that they are under-appreciated, and so will you. I did some of the following things during my career, not because I am some noble person, but because I enjoyed making myself a part of the ebb and flow of the building. I wanted to let others know that their job was just as important as anyone else's to the school (a degree makes no difference) and that I recognized and appreciated the role they played in making it all work. On the human level, there is no status. We all have a part to play and possess an equal right to walk our own path on the planet and be treated with dignity and respect.

So, when you have the time, think about doing some of the following things:

• Step in and take a teacher's morning, hall, or lunch duty when they have to meet with a parent or some emergency comes up.

• Ask department heads if you can attend one of their meetings so you can hear the current concerns of the teachers and become part of the solution, not the problem. Bring chocolate! A bag of Hershey's Kisses is a great icebreaker and an appreciated "poultice" to a long, tiring day. Open communication is the key to eradicating misunderstanding, and candy is an unexpected and great mood-elevator. I stand by it. It shows that you appreciate their time.

• When you find that a teacher is having an issue with a class, such as a need for study skills, problems with bullying, students with a lack of self-control or respect for others, etc., set a time in your calendar to go into that class and teach a lesson that will strive to bring a different perspective to the children, as well as identify those who will need one-on-one counseling.

• If you are walking through the office, and the secretary is overwhelmed with phone calls or mail for the mailboxes, offer to help. Put mail in the mailboxes, run a message to a teacher, answer the phone (if you are allowed), and if a teacher steps out into the hall because she really needs to go to the restroom, watch her class for five minutes. She doesn't have the luxury of going to the restroom anytime she wants. If a child gets hurt or in trouble when she is not present, there could be legal ramifications.

• For holidays, bring in cookies or a cake for the support staff. I enjoyed doing this for the cafeteria workers, who cook all of the time, the secretaries who are the front line for everyone who comes in the building, and the maintenance staff who clean up everybody's mess. What I wish that I could have done was do something for the bus drivers, but there were so many. However, I never ceased to tell one who might have come into the office or when I did bus duty one semester that they had to be the bravest people on the face of the earth to carry home thirty-five kids everyday on wheels in an enclosed space who are hyped up after eating *"Ho Ho's"* from lunch. They are truly under-appreciated!

• If you are walking down the hall and see a piece of paper (not a bio-hazard), pick it up and put it in the nearest trash can. If you see a kid drop a piece of trash, make him or her pick it up and throw it away. I would get quite aggravated with any kid who had the audacity to say, "Why should I? That's the janitor's job." To say the least, we would have a little "prayer meeting" about respecting the time of others and how not to make more work for them. It is yet another opportunity to teach the idea of personal responsibility to a child who needs it.

• If a child drops his books in the hall, help him pick them up, unless you are late for a meeting. Not only is it a kindness, but it demonstrates to all of the children who see it what kindness and good citizenship looks like.

• Go to the cafeteria during a time when some or all of your counselees are having lunch and walk around to say hi. Let them see you outside of your office. Kids can be totally different at lunch. So can you. Laugh and have fun. It gives you a time to connect with them on another level. Give them praise and even field some questions that don't have to end up in your office. It is a great way to build interpersonal relationships, not only with students but with the teachers who are either eating lunch in the cafeteria at that time or doing lunch duty. You can also help the cafeteria workers by making sure kids pick up their trash.

• If you see an administrator who is overwhelmed, offer to run an errand or help in some way. This is NOT "kissing up." This is doing something to help a colleague. They will probably say "no," but you can at least ask.

• Etc., etc., etc..... enough said.

It was not my intent to preach to you about doing things that are probably a part of your own nature already. It was rare that I ran into counselors who felt that anything outside of their job description was beneath them to perform, but I met a few. It was unfortunate because this kind of attitude is the antithesis of what a counselor is all about. Inevitably, that kind of attitude kept them from relating to people on a genuine level. How sad for them.

Of all of the writers who I have studied or read, I think that the playwright William Saroyan said it best in his play, <u>The Time of Your Life</u>:

"Be the inferior of no man, or of any men be superior. Remember that every man is a variation of yourself."

Chapter 24: You Don't Have to Get Burned Out, but You Probably Will—How to Resurrect Yourself Again

"I am tired. Everyone's tired of my turmoil."

"Eye and Tooth" (1964), st. 9
Robert Traill Spence Lowell

Some people believe that **burn out** is inevitable in any occupation if you are taking the job seriously and particularly if you are working in a helping profession like ours. I suppose that this is true, but maybe burn out is not the correct description for what can happen to us when we feel that our internal well has gone dry, and we wonder if we have anymore left to give.

This does happen to some counselors, no matter how many years that they have been in the profession. It is particularly common with novice counselors who are working so hard to succeed in their chosen field. The requirements of the profession make multi-tasking a mandatory tool from Day One in surviving the demands that will be placed on you by so many others.

It is all too easy to become overwhelmed while learning the job, striving to meet the expectations of administration, colleagues, parents and students, as well as reaching your own goals. The first year can sometimes feel like a trial by fire. Don't worry. Hang in there. You didn't learn to ride a bike in a day. By the end of the school year, you will have the big picture, and it will give you a much more balanced perspective of what the job entails.

I think that most of us will initially blame the job for our sense of being overwhelmed which can lead to a feeling of either temporary or long term burn out. I agree that the job is the source, but after years of being in the profession, I submit that it is an individual's reaction to the job that will determine whether or not he will reach this point, and if he can successfully resurrect himself by finding the key to refilling the dry well. The Greek Stoic philosopher Epictetus (b. 50 AD) is quoted as having said, "It's not what happens to you, but how you react to it that matters." From a personal point of view, I have incorporated this belief into my own life, and it has served me well.

It is far too easy for this job to overshadow your life, even when you are not at school. You do have to learn to leave the job at the school door each day, and you eventually will out of necessity, but the worry and concern you may feel for certain *at risk* counselees will sometimes follow you home and hide itself in the fabric of your subconscious. Even if you don't consciously think about a child, your emotions can be affected and can manifest themselves by your feeling down or depressed, more tired than usual, or feeling irritable for no apparent reason.

Day by day and child by child you come into contact with the burdens of others. Before you even know it, you feel like you are a beast of burden who is carrying more than you realized on your back, and finally the next wounded child becomes the "straw that broke the camel's back." The feeling of being physically and emotionally burned out hits you like a two by four in the back of the head, and you wonder if you can stand one more thing happening. At these moments I would ask myself how the heck I allowed myself to get to this point without recognizing the warning signs along the way.

I don't really have the quintessential answer to what causes burn out. I am sure that there are as many reasons as there are personality types among us counselors. However, I would venture to guess that one of the main underlying culprits for this state of mind is that we have either inadvertently, or perhaps by emotional osmosis, allowed ourselves to take on too much responsibility for the outcome of the choices or situations of those we have counseled. In particular, when the choice that the student or parent may make has the potential to have serious or even volatile consequences if not handled correctly, we can so easily begin to second guess ourselves and wonder if the guidance, assistance, or options that we presented to them were the best we had to offer. Since every situation is unique in its own way, we can't always think on our feet and come up with a sure fire answer for the current dilemma.

The minute we begin this thought pattern, we have automatically taken partial ownership for the outcome of someone else's choices. We then consciously or unconsciously feel that we are partially to blame if a situation has negative consequences or escalates instead of reaching a resolution. Before we can grasp what has happened, we have allowed self-imposed feelings of responsibility to contaminate our objectivity and germinate feelings of self-doubt. Over time each situation just adds one more burden on our already overburdened shoulders, and we just plain burn out. Does being overwhelmed breed "burn out" or "burn out" breed the feeling of being overwhelmed? What came first, the chicken or the egg? Who knows, but feeling burned out and overwhelmed always seemed to be wicked twins to me.

In retrospect, I suppose this happens because we are so focused on helping everyone else with their problems that we don't take the time to observe ourselves and duck when that two by four has our name written on it. By then it's too late and that burned out feeling has taken over. Sometimes we are so busy teaching others to become self-aware that we put our own awareness on the back burner until it is too late.

At this point, I highly recommend that you do a lot of good old *self-talk*. Remind yourself that you are the observer in search of <u>*possible options*</u> and not an active participant in the decision-making of other people's lives. You can present them with several game plans and cheer for them from the sidelines, but you can't run the play for them. It is much too easy to give *advice* during our sessions with counselees or parents and not phrase their options in the form of *possible choices*. Every one of us can be guilty of this, especially when we want so desperately to help someone that we find *what we have said and how we have said it* may have made the decision *for* them.

Sometimes others want us to decide for them because they either can't decide or won't decide for fear of making a mistake. The instant that we give advice instead of options, we have already "fallen down the rabbit hole" and become at least partially responsible for the outcome if that person does what we have said. It is this kind of self-imposed feeling of taking on the responsibilities of others compounded with all of the other responsibilities of the job that I personally feel is the recipe for burn out or the feeling of being so overwhelmed that the well feels dry.

Don't waste your time berating yourself for being a caring human being. Just take a step back, recognize what has happened, rebalance your emotions and objectivity, and let it all go. Take a deep breath and take what I call a *Mental Health Day*, if needed, and spend time outside of school doing the things that you love. Find an activity that you have a passion for and take a mental vacation from your *counselor self*. This will rejuvenate you.

You are the only person who can find and maintain a healthy equilibrium between your career and your personal life. Recognizing and living that balance will help to stave off burn out or be its cure before it can overtake you. To love your job is to love yourself enough to take care of yourself. Then you will have plenty in the well to help others.

Chapter 25: You are Not Perfect—Accept your Limitations

"The great act of faith is when man decides that he is not God."

Oliver Wendell Holmes, Jr.
Letter to William James—
1907

As you know, or will eventually find out, being a school counselor is a high pressure job. Depending on your school, you may have a case load of several hundred kids (my largest was about 420) with all of the built-in responsibilities for each one, as well as all of the other duties that are inherent in the job. Personal and academic issues with students, testing, school-related matters involving teachers and administrators, and ongoing parental concerns are just part of what you can have on your plate on any given day.

On some days, you will hit your stride and glide smoothly through all of the tasks that demand your attention. On other days, you will feel tired, perhaps overwhelmed, and sometimes out of sync with everything and everyone around you. This is a time when your own self-esteem can be sorely challenged. "What is wrong with me today? I *should* be able to handle all of these situations. I keep screwing up, even on small things. What am I, an idiot?"

It is that word, **should** that can make you become your own worst enemy. Even if there isn't an egotistical bone in your whole body, you know that you have enough ego to want others to recognize that you are competent in your job. With a majority of people, job performance is an intricate part of their self-esteem and how one views oneself as a capable and productive human being.

On the one hand, this is not an unreasonable expectation for anyone who has accepted the responsibility of any job. On the other hand, forcing the self-imposed and sometimes impossible expectation of what you *should* always be able to do onto your already overloaded shoulders is doing yourself a disservice and leans towards the damaging side of perfectionism.

When you combine your high expectations of yourself with the often demanding and numerous expectations of others, it is much too easy to judge yourself harshly when you realize that you have made an error in judgment (I call it an error in judgment, not a mistake—a mistake is only if you keep repeating it) and land on the receiving end of some unsympathetic and unkind criticism by another. I always found that how successfully I handled a potential knock to my self-esteem was directly proportionate to how tired I was at the time.

When you are feeling physically depleted, a negative blow to your self-esteem can more easily pierce though the armor of your own self-worth and result in your feeling even lower than you already do. This can engender self-doubt, and you then may suddenly catch yourself second, third, and fourth guessing yourself on even the simple tasks. You are then reacting to the misconception that you *should* have been able to handle that particular situation, and you are now disappointed in yourself. Don't succumb to that negative feeling just because it's there.

In addition, you can direct a lot of unnecessary and unwarranted anger towards yourself when you allow yourself to be your own worst critic. Sometimes we won't give ourselves the understanding and compassion that we would give a stranger. Oh, we can accept a mistake made by others (we expect that in our job), but heaven forbid when we make one ourselves. What will people think? Counselors are considered the "go to" people when there is a dilemma to be solved. We *should* have the answer or at least come up with one that *should* work if we are competent in our job. We are expected to be on top of everything all of the time. We can't afford to make an error. *Should* can become such a judgmental and self-destructive word.

By now it must be obvious that this is a prime example of skewed thinking. No one can be perfect, and we can't be all things to all people. You just can't avoid making errors sometimes, whether it is in your mountain of paperwork that has a deadline or wishing that you hadn't said what you did at that antagonistic parent conference that morning. Sometimes in our effort to make a situation better, we can inadvertently make it worse because we can never be sure how another person will react or interpret what we said, particularly if that person was on the defensive before she even entered the room.

Remember, too, that the school counselor can also be a convenient target when someone is looking for someone else to blame. At any moment you can find yourself in the direct line of fire, and being a human being with your own personality and emotional construct, you may react in a way that you wish you hadn't.

Although experience will reinforce your self-control, there is just no way that you aren't going to step into it sometimes, whether it is with a teacher, administrator, parent, or another counselor. You have your limitations, whether you or other people choose to recognize this fact or not, and neither you nor they should (an appropriate "should") expect you to be an onsite miracle worker.

Have enough confidence in yourself and your abilities to admit when you have either made an error or if you don't have a ready solution to a problem. If someone sits in judgment of you, it is a reflection of him or her, not on you. You do not have to make yourself a conduit for another's criticism or frustration. If a person demands perfection, feel sorry for her because she will live a life in which she will never be satisfied. For your own physical and emotional health, <u>strive for excellence but not perfection</u>. If you truly understand this and incorporate this attitude into both your work and personal life, as well as impress this concept on your counselees, you will be able to surmount almost any obstacle and avoid an unnecessary trip down the path of self-doubt.

Chapter 26: "All Mimsy were the Borogoves:" You Don't Know Everything, but You Know More than You Think

"Twas brillig, and the slithy toves
Did gyre and gimble in the wabe:
All mimsy were the borogoves,
And the mome raths outgrabe."

Lewis Carroll
"Jabberwocky", st. 1

Someday, when it has been a particularly long day, and you need a good laugh, type this Lewis Carroll quotation into your Word program and watch the Spell/Grammar Check have a nervous breakdown. On the surface it appears to be a bunch of gibberish, but is it really? Look below the surface, and you will find that these seemingly nonsensical sentences have a core structure that can compete with any other English sentence. There are subjects, verbs, and descriptive words, and with the exception of questionable punctuation, there really are two complete sentences here. Use your imagination and substitute your own words (don't worry about trying to rhyme):

"Twas chilly, and the slimy toads
Did croak and wallow in the pond:
All shiny were the lily pads,
And the insects sang outloud."

See, it makes sense, but before you begin to wonder if I have lost my mind, let me explain the reason why I just took you through this little grammar lesson.

This quotation is a perfect demonstration of how a core idea can be hidden under such embellishment that you may begin to question your skills as a counselor when a remedy is not always apparent. It can be very frustrating, and your own doubt can get in your way.

Some stories that will come into your office will be like a bad soap opera, and it will be enough of a challenge just to keep all of the details straight. You will want to shake your head and may hear yourself impulsively interject questions before you can even attempt to summarize:

"Wait a minute. Let's back up. When did this problem begin, and who said what to whom? When you say, 'she,' which of the group of four girls that were involved do you mean? Oh, that event happened a month ago, but this event happened today? You think it was the first girl who spread the rumor, but that is because a girl who *used to* be her friend told you..." On and on and on the story spins in your head as you are sinking fast in a quagmire of loosely related, and oftentimes extraneous details and emotions. I affectionately call this type of scenario *"She said, You said, They said."* It is so easy to get sidetracked by the details that you will wonder if you can come up with a viable approach to the dilemma, especially when it comes to you late in the day *(heavy sigh)*.

On the opposite end of this spectrum, you are likely to encounter a situation that is of such a serious nature that you may doubt yourself again. For example, a teacher has sent a child to you for the second time because she has found a new poem written by the girl that indicates that the child may be having suicidal thoughts. You reported this to her parents the first time (Duty to Warn), and they didn't take it seriously ("She's just being overly dramatic"). Now the new poem is much darker, you can see that the child is visibly depressed, and you know that you must inform the parents again but anticipate that their response may be the same. Now what?

Two opposite scenarios- the first taxes your already tired brain, and the second one registers a ten on your *fear meter* because you know that you can't wait for the parents to open their eyes and "Catch the Clue Bus," as my friend Winona used to say. Either way, once an issue comes through your door, it becomes your responsibility to deal with it, one way or another.

It can easily cause you to doubt yourself when there isn't always an immediate and clear-cut answer in your head. This is when you will need to sit back, take a breath, and consciously wipe away all of the exterior details to expose the core. It is the core that you will need to reach before you will be able to find the path to your best option in order to solve the dilemma. By doing so, you will have excluded all of the child's clouded emotions, as well as your own. Now, you can think and see more clearly.

The answer was always there, even if it was to consult someone else for help. In the first case, you just couldn't see the forest for the trees and needed a plan to call in the parties involved to end the ongoing rumor mill (jealousy or hurt feelings are usually at the core of this one). In the second, you just had to be proactive for the child and bring in other people and resources (school psychologist, school social worker, administration, etc.)---whatever it takes to let the parents know that you are concerned enough to consult others. They may not like the fact that the issue is now exposed because it certainly doesn't make them look good as parents, but that is not your concern. There is no confidentiality under the law of "Duty to Warn," and the child, who may also get angry with you, needs to be told this, too. If the parents think that they are being strong-armed by you, good. Sometimes people have to be shaken out of

Denial Land to do the right thing for their child before it is too late. Always err on the side of protecting the child above all else.

Your main job is to be a child advocate. Just make sure that you NEVER say to the parent or anyone else that the child is definitely suicidal. I repeat again for the umpteenth time, YOU ARE NOT A THERAPIST, and you can get into big trouble for making that statement. You can gain access to someone who is qualified, as well as obtain all kinds of support within the school system, without putting yourself in jeopardy. What you say is that you are VERY CONCERNED ABOUT THE CHILD'S CURRENT EMOTIONAL STATE, AND YOU ARE WORRIED THAT THEY **MAY** BE AT RISK. Have your documentation, like the poem, or reports by others, such as the teacher's observations, and the date that you contacted the parents the first time. Then explain that you are seeking out ways to help the parents help their child. Now, you have done the ethical thing, even if the parent rails to administration.

As a side bar, it gives you even more ammunition if the child admits that she is depressed and would accept outside help (not always possible, of course. Denial runs deep). Volley that information back to the parents while you tell them that you are researching possibilities to help their child. I openly admit that I never had any problem projecting a no-nonsense attitude with parents by telling them that their child had openly admitted to feeling depressed. What can they say now and still save face?

Let them complain to the administrator. Even better, I never had an administrator who told me to back off because of this kind of parent complaint, unless he was willing to take on the responsibility for what might happen to the child himself, and believe me, that never happened. A child's emotional problems fall under the counselor's domain, and most administrators are more than happy to bounce this kind of thing back to you. What they usually do is tell the parents to make an appointment with you or bring them over unexpectedly to see you if they just showed up at their office door out of the blue. Terrific, you've got the parents' attention. Invite the administrator to stay for your parent conference. He probably won't because he is up to his eyelids with his work, too, but it sends him the message that you are really serious. That will really get *everyone's* attention. Now, you are on record, and you got the results you wanted by creating a setting where there can be no denial.

These are just two examples of the multitude of situations that you may confront on any given day. Just don't feel intimidated if you don't have an answer instantaneously because you either feel flattened under a mound of details (Scenario 1) or because you are concerned or unclear about what course to take for a child who appears seriously at risk for self-destructive behavior (Scenario 2). YOU KNOW MORE THAN YOU THINK YOU DO. Trust yourself, use your active listening skills, gather your resources, and don't shy away from consulting with others. Helping the child is your first priority, and if you should need to ruffle a few feathers in the process, it is for the protection of the child.

Chapter 27: Seeing the Big Picture... Share and Consult with Others

"Never think that you already know all."

Ivan Petrovich Pavlov
"Bequest to the Academic Youth of Soviet
Russia" (1936)

One of the many gifts of growing older is that each year we live adds another patch of experiences to the ever-growing and ever-changing tapestry of our life. Each patch extends our vision and perspective of what life has been, what life is, and what life can be for us and others. It is having this view of the *big picture* that can be one of the strongest tools in your arsenal of skills **if** you can view these experiences objectively. Whether you are in your twenties or fifties, your life experiences, as well as your observations of other people's lives and the results of their actions, can help you in your sincere desire to help others.

One of the first things that our parents and teachers try to instill in us when we are very young is to share. I remember fighting with my sister over numerous toys. I watched my daughter and son and now my grandson and granddaughter struggle with the same life lesson. Even an only child eventually has to learn to share. Some individuals learn to do it better than others. Unfortunately, some never really learn to do this at all. It is a shame when they don't because those people will never really experience the heart-expanding feeling of unconditional giving.

To be brutally honest, I was sometimes astounded during my career at how selfish some people can be. People can be so covetous of their own work. I know that it takes a long time to do a lesson plan or create a counseling classroom presentation. Of course, I don't believe that lazy individuals should be allowed to bask in the easy life by living off of the many hours of hard work that one of their colleagues has done. If I recognized that someone never created any lesson plans or presentations herself and just leeched off of everyone else, I would not be inclined to enable such reprehensible behavior, either. However, we all have a wealth of life experiences that we can share for the benefit of our counselees, their parents or guardians, and our colleagues. By sharing our ideas and consulting with others, we can exponentially expand our own knowledge base, as well as theirs. We can *never* learn enough.

Now, let's look at the need to share information and have consultations from a completely different perspective. Always remember that your best protection is to consult with fellow school counselors and administrators when you may be dealing with an issue that could have even the slightest legal ramification to you or to your school system. That is why your professors in graduate school have stressed the importance of knowing your federal, state and local laws and counselor ethics, as well as the regulations of your individual school system. I learned this in one situation by the "school of hard knocks," and I <u>never</u> went down that road again. Luckily, there were no big ramifications for my ignorance of a particular regulation, but I got quickly *enlightened* by my principal later that day, and he was not happy. It can be an uncomfortable way to learn, especially when your ignorance of important information could have had a major effect on others. Let me explain.

My error was made while I sat in one of my first Special Education meetings as a counselor, which was attended by an Assistant Superintendent for Special Education, an assistant principal, one of the child's teachers, a social worker, a parent, and several others who were trying to decide what might be the best course to take for the benefit of this particular child. Being a "newbie" in counseling, I was asked by the social worker at the end of a very long and somewhat argumentative discussion if I thought that this particular counselee needed therapy. I innocently said, "Yes. It may be helpful" (the word *may* didn't save me!). Ohhh ! Big mistake! Within fifteen minutes after the meeting had dispersed, I was *summoned* by a phone call from the principal himself to come to his office.

Normally, a relatively easy-going man, he was furiously pacing. He had just been reamed out by the Assistant Superintendent who had attended the meeting because I had stated that the child might benefit from therapy. He then proceeded to ream me out. I deserved it. Didn't I know that if a counselor made any such statement that a child might need therapy that the County could be held responsible for paying for it? No, I didn't. Didn't I know that I was not a therapist? Yes, I did. Well then, I was not qualified to give such a recommendation, was I? It could be legally binding. And finally, I was told to NEVER make that suggestion again...and I NEVER did.

Luckily, the County didn't get stuck with the bill because of my *faux pas*, but it was a chastening experience to have my head put on stake all the way up to the School Board. Ignorance was not an excuse that I could use because it was my responsibility to know the law. If I wasn't sure, I should have consulted with someone who did know before I ever entered that meeting and opened my mouth.

Through later consulting with my director, I quickly learned the correct semantics to use when the question of therapy gets tossed in a counselor's face unexpectedly: 1) In the meeting, I should have said, "I am not qualified to make that suggestion." 2) If it is asked in a parent conference, I should say, "I am a school counselor, not a therapist. Is there *anyone* who your child feels comfortable talking to---an adult family member, an adult friend, a minister, perhaps? If **you** decide that you would like for your child to see an outside counselor or therapist, I can give you a list of local resources, and you can check with your insurance company. You can also contact the Community Services Board for information. The decision is **yours**, of course. **You** will know what is best for your own child. Let me know if you need any further information."

Always direct this question towards the parent, even if you are in a group meeting. Let me tell you. That little speech became permanently branded into my brain the minute I learned it. I shared that bit of information with anyone and everyone, especially new counselors. I hope that you do the same.

Make it a habit to keep a short stack of this resource list in your desk drawer so you won't have to leave the office to make a photocopy. We were allowed to highlight at least three therapists or offices if we had had a positive history with them in reference to certain counselees or had received very positive feedback from parents or the child. However, I still want to caution you because a parent could come back and say, " I went to one of the therapists that you *recommended*," (a misquote because you only told them that you had heard *positive feedback* about the three¬- watch your words), " and I didn't like him," thereby, pointing a finger at you if it doesn't work out. Some counselors choose to hand out the list and leave it to the insurance companies. I can understand this decision.

There will always be times when you question whether or not you are approaching the issue with the right ideas or perspective. Sometimes we are too close to the problem and doubt our objectivity. Sometimes we have never dealt with a situation like it before, and we just aren't sure how to best handle it. Sometimes we begin to doubt ourselves and wonder if our way is the best way (it will never be the *only* way). Sometimes we fear that a wrong decision could open us up to legal trouble or backfire on us or the child and possibly make a bad situation worse. The concerns go on and on. One thing is for sure. Whenever you don't feel comfortable with making a decision because that intuitive little voice inside of your head is questioning you, always, always, always consult with someone (or several *someones*) first.

However, remember to be extremely careful where and with whom you choose to discuss any counseling issue. What you may consider consultation can too easily become gossip if overheard either inside or outside of the Counseling Office by anyone who is not involved and not a professional. Consultations should be confidential in nature and include only the information that is necessary to get another person's perspective. Keep all consultations behind closed doors, and don't feel uncomfortable if you have to say to someone, "I am not at liberty to share that information with you."

What so many people on the outside don't understand is that the responsibility for making critical decisions can sometimes be an intricate part of a counselor's job, and what we do or say can have a tremendous impact on the course of a child's life. We understand and accept this, but we also have to live with it. Some counselors leave this career because they can't handle the pressure of this responsibility. That's okay. No one's job should become their nemesis. As I said earlier, counseling is not for the faint of heart.

Trust your *inner voice*. It consists of your knowledge base, your intuition, and your own experiences. When it talks to you, listen, then consult, and always share.

Chapter 28: Is it Nature, Nurture, or the Power of the Human Spirit

"Nature is often hidden; sometimes overcome; seldom extinguished."

Francis Bacon
Of Nature in Men

Is it *nature* or *nurture* that controls our destiny as human beings? This age-old question has been debated among scholars, scientists, and philosophers long before our knowledge of genetics added another log to the fire.

Since I am no expert in any of these fields of study, I won't attempt to argue one above the other. Needless to say, you as a school counselor will deal with both sides of this coin. Whether genetics drives personality or environment modifies personality, when you deal with children, you are watching a human being in the making. Each experience that the child encounters will slowly mold his view of the world and how he perceives himself and others.

Although the child is not a finished product by any means, it is important to keep in mind that both nature and nurture have already had a tremendous influence on the child before he or she has entered your office. Even if you get to know some children very well, you will never be able to fully understand the depths of who they really are and how they got that way. You are not supposed to do this, anyway. You are not a therapist or a mind reader.

Children may tell you of events in their life, show emotions, and react according to their temperament, but what they are really thinking may not be what they are feeling. They may not understand themselves. They may be overreacting. That's okay because all that we can do is work with the immediate situation, anyway. While accomplishing this, though, we are able to begin to scratch the surface of a child's individuality and get a glimpse of how nature and nurture have molded the child. Don't make any quick assumptions. Children are like flint and are in constant flux, as well--fire today and then frozen ground tomorrow. It can cause you to question your abilities as a counselor if you take it too seriously. Don't.

In my own mind, the biggest conundrum in the battle between nature and nurture has always been why some children survive their often horrendous circumstances and go on to become successful as students and adults, while others get crushed under the conditions that life has dealt them and struggle, sometimes unsuccessfully, to pick up the pieces of their decimated life. Children coming out of the same household can take very divergent paths in their reaction to the events of their life. Who can say? Is it nature or nurture or something more?

After all of my years in education and working with thousands of kids though teaching and counseling, I have observed, listened, and learned that there exists in some children a tenaciousness for life. There is a spirit in them, for lack of a better word, which refuses to be defeated by the stumbling blocks in their path. If they can't move them, they walk around them or literally jump over them, if necessary. They will not be thwarted. Is it brain chemistry (nature) or the influences of upbringing (nurture), or just plain stubbornness? One way or another, some kids have ready access to this ability and some can't seem to reach it, even though the survival instinct lives in us all.

I am not taking a flight of fancy here. Use your observation skills and intuition, and I promise you that you will see this internal strength in the depths of their eyes when you look into them. There is an indescribable quality that emanates from these children that sends you the message that no matter how despondent or defeated they feel at that moment, they will rebound and resurrect themselves again and again. It is that ethereal quality that you can recognize in them if you train yourself to see it.

You won't see it in every child, but that doesn't mean that the potential is not there. Every child has the potential to grow and learn and build survival skills. By listening and being attentive to her needs, you can help her brave the storms of her young life, while building the skills that she will need until she can escape from her environment. Hopefully, some of these skills will become life skills. Although you can only attempt to bridge a gap in her life for a moment in time, you can help a child draw upon or harness her inner strength to survive.

I have always felt that the greatest gift that I could give to a child was hope. Children haven't the life experience to know that difficult times are not forever and can be overcome. It is particularly hard for them to comprehend this when difficulty is all that they have ever known. The best that you can do is send a clear and resounding message to them that you believe in them and their ability to rise above the problems of life. It is crucial that someone tell children that they believe in them. They may never hear this at home. I have seen students make a total u-turn in their attitude when teachers and counselors reinforce this message. Even with little successes, the child will begin to believe in himself.

I left education believing that no child is a hopeless case. Every child wants to be successful no matter what cards nature or nurture has dealt him. The most hardcore, obnoxious, and inflexible kid in the world wants it most of all. He has just given up trying because he has come to expect failure. Look past the anger and see the pain in his eyes, and then try to help him develop the life skills that will at least give him a chance to make a different choice in his life.

One of the hardest things that I had to learn was that no matter what we do as counselors, some children will never reach their potential and will choose to take a hard path in life. I remember having an argument with one of my philosophy professors in college when he told me that we can't save everyone. He stated, "Some people will fall through the cracks no matter what we do to try to help." My young idealistic soul railed at this thought. He just smiled kindly because he knew that experience would teach me otherwise. True change comes from within.

Give it your all and try to keep the child from falling through the cracks while you can hopefully have some influence on him, but keep realistic. You only have these children for a short period of time in their lives. Nature and nurture were there long before you came into the picture. Work with what you observe and believe in what is possible. The rest is up to that individual.

Chapter 29: Reviewing the Path: A Road of Self-Discovery

"Each is given a bag of tools,
A shapeless mass and a book of rules,
And each must make, ere life is flown,
A stumblingblock or a steppingstone."

R. L. Sharpe
"Stumblingblock or Steppingstone", st. 2

I would imagine that it is quite obvious by now that this book has been just as much about you as it has been about discussing the many and sundry people and situations that you are likely to encounter during your counseling career. That is because, first and foremost, you bring yourself to this job, and who you are, what you think and feel, and how you control your personal thoughts and actions can dramatically impact the lives of those who you wish to help.

Since the moment you were born, you have been, and will continue to be, a work in progress. Your genetics (predestined by nature's luck of the draw), your family dynamics, your physical, emotional, and spiritual upbringing, as well as all of your positive and negative life experiences have molded you into the person you are today--a person who has chosen to live his or her life in the service of others. That's why it is so important to really understand yourself and your own motivations before you attempt to ascertain what makes someone else "tick."

Who you are and who you will become will be a composite of all that you have lived and will experience as you travel across the landscape of your life. You must take the time to identify your shadow places (we all have them) and, as much as possible, flush out any unsettled areas of your mind and heart and soul that may have been negatively influenced or perhaps damaged by certain events. Otherwise, it will be far too easy to react first and regret your response later. Remember, I found this out the hard way one day. I hope that you won't.

Please bear in mind that to strive for perfection may seem noble, but it is a trap made for fools. To live your life being afraid to make an error in judgment will turn your focus from being *other-centered* to being *self-centered*, and that will undermine your reason for being a school counselor. Instead, strive for excellence. Continue to learn and develop competence and be open to self-correcting behavior because being overly self-critical will eat away at your confidence.

It will be your attitude towards yourself, others, and how you react to the ups-and-downs of life itself that will determine to what degree you may be able to positively influence the outcome of any given situation. Who you are will shine through by the words you choose, the sincerity in your voice and facial expressions, and the confidence that you project towards those who have sought you out and are looking to you to be stronger than they currently feel.

Since neither you nor others can ever be perfect, do not expect perfect solutions. Actively listen, collect as many pieces of the puzzle as the counselee or adult may be willing to disclose, and search for options that hopefully make sense. Try not to get too frustrated if the child or parent rejects them all. Some people would rather play the Blame Game than make any effort to change themselves. But, ultimately, "All chickens come home to roost." They really do. They will have to deal with the consequences for all of their decisions or perhaps indecisions, as it may be.

If you are going to strive for anything, strive for the feeling of contentment, knowing that you have given it your all and will do your best for anyone who has been placed in your path. To accept the fact that we may never know the "why" will lead you to understand that as much as we may wish otherwise, the truth may be that *it is what it is.*

Chapter 30: The Bottom Line...

"Whatever you do for the least of my brothers, you do for (them all.)"

Jesus
Bible (interpreted and
paraphrased)
"Gospel of Matthew," 25:40

During these last four years since I retired, I have been asked by both friends and acquaintances what I have been doing with my time. When I mention that, among other things, I have been in the process of writing a book for school counselors, their responses have varied somewhere between, "That's nice" (usually the acquaintances) to, "Really, in what way?" So, here is my explanation, and it really reaches to the core of who I am and how I think. Perhaps it is also part of my philosophy of life.

I can't tell you exactly when I decided to write a book about what it is like to be a school counselor, but I think that the idea really took hold in my mind during the last several years of my profession. Realizing that my career in education had begun speeding towards its timely end, the teacher in me resurfaced and got me to thinking.

From a philosophical point of view, I thought to myself that it might be inevitable, but it seemed such a shame that after spending almost thirty-two years of my life gaining knowledge, experience, and strategies for working with children, parents, and other adults as both a teacher and a counselor, that all that I had learned was destined to go to dust. It seemed such a waste.

So I remembered what the character of Thomas Black Bull said in the Hal Borland novel, <u>When the Legends Die</u>: "Time, he thought, was like the onions he had just peeled. Layer on layer, and to get down to the heart of things you let the layers peel off, one by one." So this book was my attempt to peel off the layers of my counselor experiences one by one.

It's not that I have found "The Way of the School Counselor." Each one of you will have to make your own journey as you find your own "Counselor Within." It will be as individual as you are, and you will be amazed at how you will evolve as a person because you will be changed by every life you touch and by those lives that will touch you.

As I said at the very beginning of this book, being a counselor is not for the faint of heart. You will find yourself experiencing all of the emotions, both positive and negative, that can touch the human heart, and you will have to embrace them all and then let them go. You will have to deal with the fact that whether it was the sin of commission or omission, some parents did not do right by their child, and you will have to deal with the sometimes tragic results.

The hardest thing to accept may be when you realize that you can try to putty in the holes of a child's wounded psyche but then come to understand that there will never be a guarantee that any of what you do will stick. The damage was done long before the child reached your office, so don't carry some mantle of guilt on your shoulders if you find that no matter how hard you try, you see little or no change in a situation. Remember always that change comes from within and may require a painful journey, and some people would rather maintain the status quo than admit that there is a problem and put forth the necessary effort to make things better. That would mean that they had to admit that they may have made some incorrect decisions, and it will be much easier for them to try to blame you or someone else rather than take responsibility for their own actions.

NEVER, NEVER, NEVER allow anyone to make you either their "whipping boy" or their "fall guy." You are **NEITHER**! Demand that you be treated as the professional you are and work hard to maintain your objectivity, no matter how much hurt or compassion your heart feels for someone. You may not be able to influence some people to change, but you can teach them the first step towards making their situation better: **personal accountability**. If a child doesn't learn this in school, life will surely teach it to him on the outside. Even when the child is difficult to deal with, I will repeat what my longtime friend and fellow school counselor Lenny always said: "Treat each child in a way that you would want your own child to be treated."

And for those possible times when you are sitting at your desk at the end of the day, staring at the wall in front of you and wondering if you have ever really made a difference, I leave you with a story that is usually attributed to an anthropologist named Loren Eiseley (1907-1977) and has been adapted in many forms from his book <u>The Star Thrower</u>. It pretty well sums up what I feel should be the attitude of all educators, not just school counselors. Here is one adaptation that I have paraphrased:

The Starfish Story

Once upon a time, there was a wise man who used to go to the ocean in the morning to do his writing.

One day, while he was walking along the shore, he looked down the beach and saw a human figure moving like a dancer. Fascinated, he walked faster to catch up. As he got closer, he realized that the figure was a young man, and that what he was doing was not dancing at all. Instead, the young man was reaching down to the shore, picking up small objects, and throwing them into the ocean.

As he came closer, he called out to the young man, saying, "Hello! May I ask what it is that you are doing?"

The young man paused, looked up, and replied, "Throwing starfish into the ocean."

"I don't mean to be rude," said the wise man, "but may I ask you, why are you throwing starfish into the ocean?"

The young man replied, "The sun is up and the tide is going out. If I don't throw them back into the ocean, they will die."

Upon a moment's reflection, the wise man commented, "But, young man, do you not realize that there are miles of beach, and there are starfish all along every mile? You can't possibly make a difference!"

At this, the young man smiled, bent down, picked up yet another starfish, and threw it into the ocean. As they both watched the starfish hit the water and disappear from sight, the young man turned and said, "It made a difference for that one."

****

The desire to help others is truly a gift. Share it with all of those who are willing to accept it. This was my intention for writing this book. Strive to be all that you can be, but remember to be as kind and patient with yourself as you are with others.

And now, as my daughter used to say during high school after entering my office and tapping me on the shoulder like a wayward little woodpecker, "Time to go!"

Godspeed in all of your endeavors.

Works Cited

American School Counselor Association. Ethical Standards for School Counselors. "Dual Relationships." Section A4. Revised 2010. USA: American School Counselor Association, 2010, http://asca2.timberlakepublishing.com//files/EthicalStandards2010.pdf

Bartlett, John. Familiar Quotations: A Collection of Passages, Phrases, and Proverbs. 14th. Edition. USA: Little, Brown and Company, 1968, Print.

Bible, "Gospel of Matthew, 25:40. King James Version. NY: American Bible Society. Instituted in 1816, Print

Borland, Hal. When the Legends Die. Lippincott Publishers, 1963, Print.

Dalai Lama. Authors Quotations. Brainy Quote. April 10, 2011. http://www.brainyquote.com/authors/d/dalia_lama. html.

Eisley, Loren. "The Starfish Story." Adapted from The Star Thrower. USA: A Harvest Book, 1979.

Epictetus, Author's Quotations. Brainy Quote. August 25, 2011. http://www.brainyquote.com/authors/e/epictetus149126html.

Gelbart, Larry. MASH. USA: CBS, 1970, Television.

Gray, Eden. A Complete Guide to the Tarot. NY: Crown Publishers, 1970, Print.

McKinney-Vento Act, Title VII-B of the McKinney-Vento Homeless Assistance Act, Amended by the No Child Left Behind Act, 2001, Education for Homeless Children and Youth Program. http://www2.ed.gov/programs/homeless/guidance.pdf.

Negreanu, Daniel. World Poker Tour. World Series of Poker. USA: ESPN, 2009, Statement made on Television.

Paige, Satchel, The Official Satchel Paige Quote Page. March 1, 2011. http://www.satchel paige.com/quote2.html.

Saroyan, William. <u>The Time of Your Life</u>. NY: Harcourt Brace, 1939.
http:/www.goodreads.com/quotes/show/23865

Wictionary. www.wictionary.org

<u>Wikiquote.</u> Yiddish Proverbs. April 10, 2011.
http://en.wikiquote.org/wiki/Yiddish_proverbs

Wilson, Hugh. <u>WKRP in Cincinnati</u>. USA: CBS, 1978, Television